D1389682

THE A TO Z OF RUGBY

Written by
Paul Morgan & Adam Hathaway

THE A TO Z OF
RUGBY

This edition first published in the UK in 2009
By Green Umbrella Publishing

© Green Umbrella Publishing 2009

www.gupublishing.co.uk

Publishers Jules Gammond and Vanessa Gardner

All rights reserved. No part of this work may be reproduced or
utilised in any form or by any means, electronic or mechanical,
including photocopying, recording or by any information
storage and retrieval system, without prior written permission
of the publisher.

Printed and bound in Italy

ISBN: 978-1-906635-28-2

The views in this book are those of the author but they are general views
only and readers are urged to consult the relevant and qualified specialist for
individual advice in particular situations.

Green Umbrella Publishing hereby exclude all liability to the extent permitted
by law of any errors or omissions in this book and for any loss, damage or
expense (whether direct or indirect) suffered by a third party relying on any
information contained in this book.

All our best endeavours have been made to secure copyright clearance
for every photograph used but in the event of any copyright owner being
overlooked please address correspondence to Green Umbrella Publishing
The Old Bakehouse, 21 The Street, Lydiard Millicent, Swindon SN5 3LU

Contents

Australia

▶ Action unfolds during the 2007 quarter final between Australia and England.

For a comparatively small nation, Australia has a staggering record of sporting success in pursuits staged anywhere from the swimming pool and athletics track to the rugby ground and cricket pitch.

This pre-eminence is put down to many factors, most notably the healthy outdoor lifestyle enjoyed by Australian youngsters and their famous refusal to bend in the competitive arena. Whether the game is dominoes down the local or a World Cup final, Australians always want to win.

Their success in rugby union is remarkable. They have won the World Cup twice (in 1991 and 1999) and with the wind in the right direction they may have made it three wins out of a possible six when losing to England in the 2003 final. Bear in mind that rugby union in most states of Australia is not the first-choice winter sport of many, coming second, third or fourth to rugby league, Aussie Rules and more recently the ubiquitous soccer. Thus, their success is even more admirable or envy-inducing depending on which side of the equator you come from.

However the love of the 15-man code down under was in evidence when they staged the 2003 World Cup. Over two million paying spectators turned up to watch a tournament that stretched the length and breadth of the country, and even "non-union" states embraced the event.

▼ Australia's first ever international match vs the Lions, 1899.

it was run from Twickenham until the formation of the New South Wales and Queensland Rugby Unions in 1881 and 1892 respectively.

Seven years later, Australia played their first Test match when representatives of these unions teamed up to take on a touring side from the British Isles. The Australians marked their debut in international rugby with a 13-3 win in Sydney but lost the remaining three Tests to go down 3-1 in the series. In 1904, when the British returned, the visitors won all three Tests in the series. Then, in 1908, the "Wallabies" were born.

The first Australian rugby club was at Sydney University, formed in 1864, and in 1874 there were enough teams in the area to form a competition. Thus the Southern RFU was established, though

The Australians toured the United Kingdom and North America and as they followed the New Zealand tourists, who were dubbed the "All Blacks", it was, according to the Australian Rugby

▼ Mark Ella, star
of the Wallabies
1984 Grand Slam
touring side.

Union, suggested by members of the press that they should be called the "Rabbits". The team rejected this as the rabbit was an imported pest, so they settled on being named after the native wallaby instead.

They were no rabbits on the field however and the Wallabies won 32 of 38 games on that trip. They also took an Olympic gold medal back home after beating England, represented by Cornwall, 32–3 in the final in London. The effect of the First World War and the increased influence of rugby league saw union go backwards for a few years up to 1928 when the Queensland Rugby Union started up again.

In 1929, Australia beat New Zealand in all three Tests for the first time. They also adopted green and gold as their official colours and in 1934 they won the Bledisloe Cup for the first time, beating their old rivals New Zealand 25-11 in the first Test in Sydney and drawing the second 3-3.

After the Second World War, the Wallabies embarked on a triumphant tour of the United Kingdom and America. Considering the modern infatuation with defence, it is interesting to note that in four Tests against the home unions the Australian line was not crossed once. At the end of the trip, Australia were invited to join the International Rugby Board. They have hardly looked back since and their teams have thrilled spectators the world over.

In 1979, they won the Bledisloe Cup for the first time since 1949 and in 1981 Mark, Gary and Glen Ella became the first three brothers to be picked for the same Wallaby squad. Fly-half Mark was the star of the show and scored a try in each Test of the Wallabies' Grand Slam tour of the United Kingdom in 1984, repeating his achievement of 1977-78 when he toured the British Isles with the Australian Schoolboys' side.

He retired at the ridiculously early age of 25, but is still considered one of the finest No 10s ever to

◀ Nick Farr-Jones holds up the Webb Ellis Cup after victory in 1991 over England.

lace up a pair of boots. The 1984 tour was a vindication of the Australian board's policy of reviewing their coaching philosophy after a lean time in the early 1970s.

The first Rugby World Cup took place, unfortunately without Mark Ella, in 1987 and was hosted in Australia and New Zealand as those two countries

▲ The great John Eales' career ended on a high after Australia beat the 2001 Lions.

the semi-final in Dublin, the brilliant Australian wing David Campese scored one try and made another for centre Tim Horan to put New Zealand to the sword 16-6 and set up a Twickenham finale against England.

Campese did not get a chance to shine in a poor final, but the Wallabies were canny and defensively sound enough to win 12-6 and captain Nick Farr-Jones lifted the trophy to the grey London skies.

In 1999, Australia were easily the best side in the competition, winning the final 35-12 against France and providing a fitting international farewell for Horan, his long-time midfield partner Jason Little and flanker David Wilson.

The core of the side survived to defeat the British Lions 2-1 in 2001 and send the legendary second-row and captain John Eales into retirement a happy man.

They narrowly missed out on victory in the 2003 World Cup final when beaten by a last minute Jonny Wilkinson drop goal; and it was Jonny again who shattered their dreams with his successful penalties contributing to a 12-10 defeat in the quarter-finals of the 2007 World Cup.

had floated the idea of a global showpiece tournament in the first place.

The Wallabies made serene progress to the semi-finals and looked set for a place against New Zealand, the eventual winners, in the final. However, fate, or more accurately the French full-back Serge Blanco, intervened with one of the most famous tries in rugby history and the Australians lost a pulsating semi-final 30-24.

They made amends in the next tournament in 1991 which was spread over the British Isles and France. In

Barbarians

One team sums up the romance and spirit of rugby union. Those famous men in their black and white hoops – the Barbarians!

The Barbarians, who are a United Nations of Rugby, represent a glorious concept. They embody the spirit of rugby, brought to life by the vision and enthusiasm of one man, William Percy Carpmael.

Invitations to play are sent to players from all corners of the rugby world as long as they adhere to the Barbarians motto; "Rugby football is a game for gentlemen in all classes but never for a bad sportsman in any class."

Inspired by his personal playing experiences with both Blackheath and Cambridge University, Carpmael's dream was to spread good fellowship amongst all rugby football players. The dream became reality on 27 December 1890 at Friary Field, Hartlepool.

In 1890, after the rugby season had finished in March, Carpmael took the Southern Nomads – mainly composed of players from Blackheath – on a tour to the north. As legend has it, in a restaurant in Bradford, the concept was agreed upon over supper. He saw the team as an opportunity to play with friends from various clubs who were normally opponents.

He loved the culture behind the rugby tour and came up with the idea of regular short tours involving players of the highest skill levels.

In Carpmael's vision this side needed no ground, clubhouse or subscription and membership was by invitation only, but that hasn't stopped them becoming one of the most revered sporting institutions in the world.

They are a scratch side, with

▲ The 1973 Barbarians pose before their famous match against New Zealand.

BARBARIANS

▼ Gareth Edwards is chaired off the pitch after the 1973 victory.

players from all over the world, wearing the famous black and white hoops, black shorts, and their own socks, to exemplify the nations and clubs involved.

The only criteria a player must fulfil to receive an invitation from the Barbarians is; that the player's rugby is of a good standard and that they behave themselves on and off the field. "There is no discrimination on the basis of a player's race, colour or creed," the club explain, "and since 1890, players from 23 different countries have worn the jersey. Once invited a player becomes a life member of the club."

Winning and losing are never the most important things in a

Barbarians match, as it is definitely a case of how you played the game, with flair and an eye not on the scoreboard but the try line.

Every rugby supporter, no matter which side they follow tends to be a supporter of the Barbarians and they have an incredibly successful Friends organisation and a website;

www.barbarianfc.co.uk.

As a result of many scintillating performances, the Barbarians won respect worldwide and on 31 January 1948 they were invited to play the Australians at Cardiff Arms Park in the final match of that tour. It was their first against international opposition. The battle captured the

▲ Jeremy Guscott playing for the Barbarians against England at Twickenham in 2001.

► Kris Chesney of the Barbarians jumps for the line-out ball during the friendly match against Ireland, May 2008.

imagination of millions and drew a capacity crowd of 45,000.

So successful was the fixture that it became tradition for Australia, New Zealand or South Africa – whichever was touring the UK – to tackle the Barbarians in "The Final Challenge."

Those great matches against touring sides hit a high point in 1973 when the Barbarians took on New Zealand, at Cardiff Arms Park. On that day Gareth Edwards finished off a length of the field move, to score one of the most famous tries in the history of the game. THAT try went through seven pairs of hands, encapsulating everything about Barbarians rugby. An equally acclaimed victory was achieved in 1961 when the Barbarians played the South African Springboks captained by Avril Malan. The Springboks were unbeaten on their tour of Great Britain and Ireland.

In their last match of the tour the Barbarians held on to a 6-0 lead thanks to some fierce tackling and carried off the Springbok head – a trophy traditionally presented by the South African tourists to the first side to beat them when on tour.

Hundreds of internationals have represented the Barbarians but the most

prolific was AJF (Tony) O'Reilly, the Lions and Ireland wing, who made his debut as a Barbarian in 1955, helping the club to a 6-3 win against Cardiff. He went on to represent the club a record 30 times, scoring a record 38 tries, making his final appearance against Swansea eight years later in 1963.

When the game turned professional in 1995 it did threaten the existence of the Barbarians. They have lost many of their traditional fixtures against club sides. However, with great players like Jonah Lomu, Zinzan Brooke and Agustin Pichot backing the club and the presence of its spiritual leader, and president, Mickey Steele-Bodger never far away they now have a huge, and respected, presence in the world game.

Today the Barbarians hold such an important place in our game that other countries, like New Zealand, France, South Africa and Australia have set up their own Barbarians side, the New Zealand version coming to Twickenham in December 2003 to take on the newly crowned world champions, England.

One of England's greatest players, Jeremy Guscott, ended his international career with the Barbarians in the summer of 2001 on one of their now regular summer tours against the best of Britain and Ireland.

"There was to one final hurrah (in my career)," Guscott recalls in his autobiography, "and what a crack it was.

"It was good fun meeting up with the boys, just like an old-fashioned tour where the social side is as important as the playing side.

"I wish the Baa-Baas had had these tours before. I know it would have been nigh on impossible because of the way the game was structured and because the boys had day jobs, but it was one hell of an experience, one hell of a way to finish off."

Rather than allow professionalism to kill off the Barbarians the grand old club feeds off tradition and the desire of players and supporters to hold on to just one part of the amateur game.

This sense of traditional values was gloriously celebrated when the British Olympic Association arranged for the Barbarians to play Australia at Wembley in December 2008 as part of the centenary celebrations of the first London Olympic Games where Australia defeated a Great Britain (Cornwall) side in the final 32-3.

Calcutta Cup

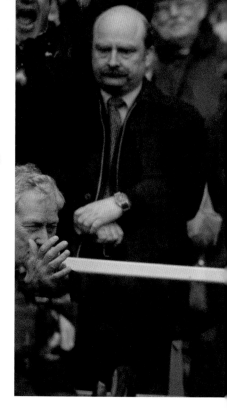

Scotland and England are the oldest rivals in international rugby having played their first Test match in 1871 at Raeburn Place in Edinburgh – a game that ended in victory to the Scots by a goal and a try to a goal.

Nowadays, the winning captain, in the annual fixture played during the Six Nations, receives the Calcutta Cup, an ornate trophy made from melted-down silver Indian rupees that has a history almost as interesting as the fixture itself.

On Christmas Day in 1872, a game of rugby was played in Calcutta between a 20-man side representing England and 20 men of Scotland, Ireland and Wales. This led to the formation of the Calcutta Football Club a year later.

However, the club was reluctantly disbanded in 1878 due to a lack of opposition and the 13 rupees that were left in the kitty were used to make a trophy that stands 18" high, has three cobras as handles and an elephant on top. The cup was then donated to the Rugby Football Union to be played for by England and Scotland each year.

The first Calcutta Cup match in 1879 ended in a 3-3 draw but England

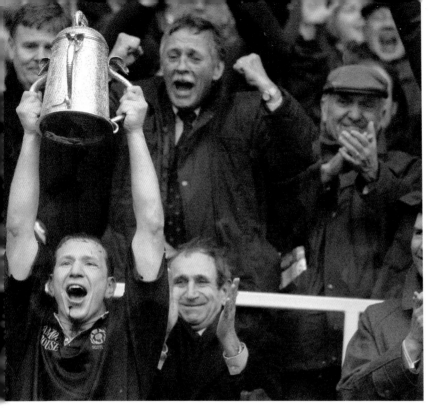

◀ Bloodied Scottish captain Andy Nicol lifts the 2000 Calcutta Cup.

took possession of the trophy when they won in Manchester a year later. A tradition was born and over the years the match has thrown up some of the greatest rugby seen on the international stage as well as its share of controversy on and off the pitch.

Nothing is guaranteed to get the Scots up for a match more than squaring up to the "Auld Enemy" and England have returned from Murrayfield with a bloody nose on more than one occasion – notably in 1990 and 2000 when they headed north in search of European Grand Slams only to pass back over Hadrian's Wall with their

▲ Clive Woodward calls the shots for England during their 1980 Grand Slam season.

tails between their legs.

It was the Scots who were the first to be left red-faced though when they were so confident of winning in 1897 that they neglected to take the trophy with them to Manchester. Sport has a habit of bringing sides down to earth and England, led by Ernest Taylor, ran out 12-3 victors.

In 1925, Murrayfield staged its first ever international, fittingly a Calcutta Cup fixture, and the Scots used the occasion to claim their first ever Grand Slam. They ground out a 14-11 win to complete a clean sweep after victories over Ireland (14-8), Wales (24-14) and France (25-4). They did not repeat the feat for another 59 years.

In 1980, England travelled to Murrayfield looking for a Slam of their own. Captained by second-row Bill Beaumont they had a centre in their side called plain Mr Clive Woodward – whatever happened to him?

Beaumont's side were clear favourites and duly did the business, winning 30-18 with winger John Carleton scoring a hat-trick of tries. The next time the red rosers ventured north in search of a Grand Slam it all panned out rather differently in 1990.

England, led by Will Carling, were perceived to be haughty and arrogant and everyone bar the Scotland fans had ignored the fact that David Sole's side were chasing a Slam of their own. Sole set the tone for the afternoon with his long, slow march on to the pitch at the head of his team.

Scotland took an early lead before being pegged back by a Jeremy Guscott try just before the break. Then Tony Stanger delivered the killer blow for the Scots in the second half beating the defence to touch down. England lost their heads completely, were rattled by the Scots and ended up arguing amongst themselves. Craig Chalmers' boot did the rest and to the strains of "Flower of Scotland" from the crowd the hosts won 13-7, took their third Grand Slam and cross-border bragging rights for the next year. Sole said afterwards; "We were going for the same prize but in the English media it was as if it wasn't even a contest."

Not all of the most famous Calcutta

Cup stories occur on the pitch and in 1988 the after-match celebrations made front and back page news. It's a good job there was something to talk about because the match itself was a desperate 9–6 win for England. Scottish flanker John Jeffrey and England No 8 Dean Richards livened up the Monday morning papers when it was disclosed that they had over-indulged in the post-match hospitality and reportedly had an impromptu game of football with the Calcutta Cup through the streets of Edinburgh in the early hours. The cup was renamed the "Calcutta Plate" by the tabloids, both players were severely disciplined and a Scottish silversmith repaired the damage.

Back on the pitch in 1994 the Scots had an agonising near-miss in the fixture

▼ Back Row England players, (left to right) Lawrence Dallaglio, Chris Jones and Richard Hill pose with the Calcutta Cup after England's 43-3 destruction of Scotland at Murrayfield, 2004.

▲ Scotland celebrate with the Calcutta Cup following their victory at Murrayfield, March 2008.

Scottish psyche because they demolished their visitors' Grand Slam hopes again in the Calcutta Cup match of 2000 at Murrayfield. England were again well-fancied and were cruising after Lawrence Dallaglio went over to score.

However the rains came, England failed to adapt and Duncan Hodge scored all of Scotland's points in a memorable 19-13 win.

England cruised to victory in 2005, winning 43-22 to present new skipper Martin Corry with a trophy but in 2006 England's Six Nations campaign started to go wrong in the Calcutta Cup game. England won almost double the possession but still lost 18-12, sparking wild celebrations in the Scottish capital, as the men in dark won for only the second time against England since 1990.

The following year saw Jonny Wilkinson notch 27 points, a record score by a player in a Calcutta Cup game, helping England to a 42-20 victory; whilst Scotland gained revenge a year later with a narrow win.

Form often goes out of the window with this fixture and if you are ever tempted to have a bet on a Calcutta Cup match, do yourself a favour and keep your money in your pocket!

losing 15-14 in Edinburgh. Carling's England arrived in the Scottish capital with a win over the All Blacks under their belt but were soon under the cosh when Rob Wainwright dashed through to score. England were reliant on the boot of Jon Callard for their points but looked to be sunk when Gregor Townsend dropped a goal in the 79th minute. However in injury time Callard knocked over a penalty, England breathed a sigh of relief and Scottish captain Gavin Hastings broke down in tears when interviewed on television.

Six years on, the boot was on the other foot. It must be cocking a snoot at the English that does something to the

Dragons

O f the four home nations, Wales has arguably the strongest rugby heritage and there is no denying the game is a vital ingredient in the life-blood of the nation.

The game was introduced to Wales at Lampeter College in the mid-19th century using the Rugby School rules but it was the selection of the first official Welsh team by Richard Mullock to face England in 1881 that is seen as the birth of Welsh rugby union.

Unfortunately, it was like lambs to the slaughter. Led by the Australian-born, Cambridge University undergraduate James Bevan, Wales were humiliated as England won by seven goals, one dropped goal and six tries to nil – or 82-0 by current scoring values.

It wasn't until 1890, at the seventh attempt, that Wales achieved the "Holy Grail" and finally beat England. A try,

then worth one point, by "Buller" Stadden at Crown Flat, Dewsbury, won the day and the legendary Arthur Gould's team were ready to take the game by storm.

The first Triple Crown came in 1893 and was the launch pad for the first "Golden Era" when Wales dominated the world game. The Maoris, the first touring team in the UK, had been beaten in 1888 and Dave Gallaher's otherwise all-conquering New Zealand "All Blacks" were beaten 3-0 in 1905 thanks to a try by Teddy Morgan. More than any other in the history of the game, that incredible match, the only fixture lost by the All Blacks, helped to turn rugby union into a game of global interest.

▲ Barry John kicks on during Wales' 1972 game against France at Cardiff Arms Park.

This golden period included the first Grand Slam won by any country and a record winning run of 11 games as Wales remained unbeaten between March 1907 and January 1910. When Rob Howley's side of 1999 matched that feat they did it in eight months. There were Grand Slams in 1908, 1909 and 1911, Triple Crowns in 1900, 1902, 1905, 1908, 1909 and 1911 and those victories over New Zealand in 1905 and Australia in 1908. The Dragons had arrived as a major force in the world game.

The 1920s and 1930s were harder times with less noticeable achievements.

There was, however, a first win at the new home of English rugby, Twickenham, in 1933 after 23 years of trying and a second win over the mighty "All Blacks" in Cardiff in 1935, 13-12. International rugby shut down for much of the 1940s because of the Second World War and only four players crossed the seven year gap – the incomparable Haydn Tanner, Bunner Travers, Les Manfield and Howard Davies.

The 1950s brought Welsh rugby right back to the forefront of the world game with Grand Slams in 1950 and 1952, under the captaincy of John Gwilliam, and a third win over New Zealand in Cardiff in 1953. Bleddyn Williams, Jack Matthews, Cliff Morgan, Roy John, Ken Jones, Billy Williams, Rhys Williams, Bryn Meredith and Clem Thomas became household names and revered opponents across the world while playing for the British & Irish Lions. The Grand Slam of 1950, crowned with a 21-0 win over France in Cardiff, ended a 39 year honours drought.

It was 19 years after the success of 1952 before the sixth Grand Slam of 1971 heralded the dawn of the second "Golden Era". Clive Rowlands' 1965 side delivered the Triple Crown, but it wasn't until he had taken over from David Nash as only the second Welsh coach in 1969 that the good times began to roll again. Players like Gareth Edwards, Barry John, Mervyn Davies, John Taylor, JPR Williams, Gerald Davies and John Dawes emerged to take not only Welsh rugby, but also the British game to the top of the world with some scintillating performances throughout the 1970s.

The 1969 Triple Crown paved the way for the 1971 Grand Slam, which was won by a team widely regarded as the greatest side ever to wear the Welsh jersey. The "Super Seventies" included Grand Slams in 1971, 1976 and 1978 and Triple Crowns in 1971, 1976, 1977, 1978 and 1979. Had the game in Ireland in 1972 not been cancelled, that otherwise undefeated campaign could have ended with another Grand Slam.

There were 11 Welshmen in the victorious 1971 Lions Test side in New Zealand and six Welsh players in the victorious 1974 Lions Test side in South Africa. Other Welsh greats from this era were Phil Bennett, Geoff Wheel, Allan Martin, the Pontypool front-row – Charlie Faulkner, Bobby Windsor and

▲ The Welsh Grand Slam winning side of 1950.

Graham Price – and Steve Fenwick.

The 1980s saw the WRU celebrate its 100th anniversary in the 1980-1981 season; the Rugby World Cup make its bow in 1987, with Richard Moriarty's Welsh side finishing third by beating Australia; the emergence of Jonathan Davies as a world class player; and a Triple Crown in 1988.

The 1990s saw professionalism enter rugby union for the first time when the former WRU Chairman Vernon Pugh pronounced in Paris in 1995 that the game would be "open". Neil Jenkins became the first international player to break the 1,000 points barrier and the biggest transformation of the decade was that of the old Cardiff Arms Park into the Millennium Stadium in time

DRAGONS

▲ Flanker Martyn Williams gets the ball out from a ruck in the Six Nations match against France, March 2008.

▶ Captain Ryan Jones holds Six Nations trophy, 2008.

to host the 1999 Rugby World Cup. After 113 years of hosting international rugby, the spiritual home of Welsh rugby, the Arms Park, was torn down and recreated into one of the most magnificent rugby venues in the world.

More recently the team has also performed magnificently with Grand Slams in 2005 and 2008 as captains Gareth Thomas and Ryan Jones accepted the coveted Six Nations Trophy after their epic final day wins over Ireland and France respectively.

The unbridled celebrations of these victories by an adoring public truly underlined the status of rugby as Wales' national sport.

England

When Jonny Wilkinson's drop goal sailed through the Sydney posts in November 2003 to land England their first World Cup, it was the culmination of one of the most professionally painstaking campaigns ever put together by an English sporting side. It was also the complete opposite of the way the Rugby Football Union started in 1871.

Then, on 26 January, 21 English clubs met at the Pall Mall Restaurant near Trafalgar Square, to form a ruling body. There should have been representatives from 22 teams, but the man from Wasps went to the wrong watering hole, stayed there and missed the meeting. Some harsh critics of the authorities may say this absent-mindedness was a taste of things to come.

England played in the first ever rugby international, against Scotland in March 1871, and enjoyed success in the International championship from its formation in 1883 to the mid-1890s.

However, there was trouble in the air and the disagreement between the RFU and its northern members over compensation for loss of earnings for

▲ The England and Scotland teams that took part in the first ever international in 1871.

▲ Eric Evans, captain of England's 1957 Grand Slam winning side.

▶ Bill Beaumont playing against Scotland in 1980, England's Grand Slam year.

players led to the split in 1895 that led to the formation of the Northern Union – which would become the Rugby League. English rugby union lost a lot of players to the new code and would not regain the International championship until 1910, the year when England played Tests at Twickenham for the first time.

By the time of the 1924 Calcutta Cup match, the ground held 43,000 spectators and its development was matched by that of the England side which played some of its best rugby during the period. Despite losing many players in the First World War when the RFU urged all of its men to sign up for action, the English won the Grand Slam in 1921, 1923, 1924 and 1928. They would not win another for 29 years until Eric Evans led his side to a clean sweep.

After Evans' success in 1957, it was a further 23 years before England, led by Bill Beaumont and boasting players such as Fran Cotton, Clive Woodward and Roger Uttley, won the Slam again in 1980.

The years between the Evans and Beaumont successes were particularly barren for the English. They did not win in Cardiff between 1963 and 1991.

There were highlights, though. John Pullin's 1972 tourists beat South Africa away and a year later the hooker led his team to victory over the All Blacks in Auckland. These glitches apart, the period was marked by selectorial incompetence. In 1979 the North, watched by the chairman of the English selectors Budge Rogers, beat the touring New Zealanders 21-9 at Otley. Running the show from fly-half was

Alan Old (the brother of the English Test cricketer Chris). But rather than play Old in the Test match the week after, the selectors picked Les Cusworth and broke up the North's back-row. New Zealand were there for the taking but England missed their chance.

Mike Davis' appointment as England coach heralded a revival that ended in Beaumont's team winning the Grand Slam, but it was only as the 1990s approached that England began to punch their weight and make the most of their huge playing resources.

In 1988 Will Carling was made England's captain, starting his reign with a win over Australia at Twickenham and becoming one of the most recognisable sporting faces in England.

When England blew the Grand Slam against Scotland in 1990, in a match notable for the squabbling among many of the England players, Carling's leadership was questioned. He answered the critics by leading England to Slams in 1991,

1992 and 1995, and taking them to the 1991 World Cup final.

Carling also led England at the 1995 World Cup in South Africa where they were knocked out in the semi-finals by the incredible hulking form of Jonah Lomu. Carling himself nearly did not get that far. Before the tournament he was quoted as saying the RFU was run by "57 old farts". The quote was apparently meant to be off the record, but it was too good for the makers of a documentary to leave out of the trailers for the programme. Carling was sacked but the RFU reinstated the skipper after he had apologised. Carling was captain

▲ Will Carling's first game as England captain, a 28-19 victory over Australia 1988.

▲ Rugby World Cup champions in 2003.

tabloid. The road to the 2003 World Cup in Australia was littered with history-making results, but the journey was far from smooth.

In November 2000, fresh from a last-minute win over Australia, the England players threatened to strike over money. The players were unhappy that their match fees were not guaranteed but included a win bonus. Woodward was incandescent and expelled the players from the team hotel, saying he would play himself against Argentina the following Saturday if the players did not see sense. Eventually, the situation was sorted out and the team beat Argentina and South Africa in successive weeks.

Woodward's side had several Grand Slam flops but were gathering momentum. They supplied the bulk of the 2001 Lions squad, beat the Southern Hemisphere teams regularly at Twickenham and destroyed Ireland to claim their first Slam in 2003.

Away wins against New Zealand and Australia followed and ensured

until 1996 when he stepped down after leading England to 44 wins from 59 games in charge.

Clive Woodward became England coach in 1997 and two years later he urged everyone to "judge me on the World Cup" after a series of indifferent results. England were drop-kicked out of the tournament by South African fly-half Jannie de Beer in the quarter-final in Paris, but Woodward survived to continue his revolution within English rugby.

Martin Johnson, who had captained the victorious 1997 Lions, was Woodward's captain after Lawrence Dallaglio was forced to resign following allegations of drug-taking in a Sunday

THE A TO Z OF RUGBY

England went into the World Cup back in Australia as the world's top team. They spluttered once or twice during the tournament, but Johnson would not be denied the crowning glory of his brilliant career. His retirement and Wilkinson's absence while recovering from a shoulder operation were contributory factors to England's disappointing Six Nations campaign in 2004. That disappointment turned to one of the most disappointing periods in recent English rugby history as they finished fourth in both the 2005 and 2006 Six Nations.

The 2007 defence of the cup in France got off to a poor start, with a below par victory over the United States and a heavy 36-0 defeat to South Africa leaving the holders on the brink of elimination at the group stage. Improved performances against Samoa and Tonga saw England again reach the knockout stages as pool runners-up, before a surprise 12-10 defeat of Australia in Marseille and a narrow 14-9 victory over the host nation France carried England to a second successive final appearance. The final was played in Paris against South Africa, who won a closely contested match by 15 points to 6.

England finished runners-up of the 2008 Six Nations but hopes for the future were significantly raised during the year with the appointment of the legendary Martin Johnson as head coach.

▲ Action from the 2007 Rugby World Cup final.

▲▲ New manager Martin Johnson (centre) with his coaching staff.

France

▶ The French team celebrate after their amazing 43-31 1999 Rugby World Cup semi-final victory over New Zealand.

France represent two extremes to the rugby fan. On their day they can beat anyone in a style to gladden the hearts of the purist but on an off-day they can be a complete shambles. In the 1999 World Cup semi-final against New Zealand, they turned round a 24-10 deficit to win 43-31 in a contest billed by some pundits as the greatest game ever played. In the final against Australia a week later, they barely turned up and John Eales, the Wallaby captain, threatened to take his side off the pitch in protest at the rough-house tactics of the French.

Rugby was introduced to France by a group of English merchants who formed Le Havre Athletic Club. The club still exists though, shamefully, they now play soccer! Nonetheless they have retained their original colours of light and dark blue that were representative of Oxford and Cambridge universities.

The first French championship was held in 1892, with the Racing Club de France beating Stade Francais, though the "Stadistes" got their revenge the following year in a repeat of the final. The game spread swiftly through France with a Scotsman taking it to Bordeaux and a Welshman forming a club in Bayonne. Soon the entire south of the country was converted.

France won the Olympic gold medal for rugby in 1900, beating Germany in the final, but the Federation Francaise

▲ France take on England in Paris in the 1958 Five Nations.

de Rugby was not formed until 1920. Before the birth of the FFR, the national team were busy but not successful – in 28 internationals before the First World War they won just once, shocking Scotland in 1911.

In 1920, the French won their first international away from home, beating the Irish, and gave England a scare at Twickenham. But their improvement was stalled in February 1931 when the IRB announced that all French fixtures would be abandoned at the end of that season. Their suspension was a high-handed response from the IRB to the way rugby was run in France, with players reputedly being paid to play and crowd trouble breaking out at some games. Twelve French clubs split from their federation and their 14-13 win over England was the last championship game for the French for 16 years. They eventually settled their differences with the IRB and were readmitted after the Second World War.

Rugby in France made great strides in the years after the war and in 1958, led by Lucien Mias, they won a series in South Africa for the first time. But their rows with the authorities rumbled on – they were accused of choosing rugby

▲ The French Grand Slam winning team of 1968 before their game against Ireland.

in the French XV of the 20th century when it was announced at the turn of the millennium.

The late 1960s and early 1970s were a golden period for the French. They won the Five Nations in 1967 and 1968 and shared the title in 1970 and 1973. During this time, their biggest rivals in European rugby were the Welsh and the two countries shared some epic battles. Jo Maso, now the team French manager, was one of the stars of the show along with Guy Camberabero, Claude Dourthe and Pierre Villepreux.

In the 1980s, France were consistently the best side in Europe and won Grand Slams in 1981 and 1987 under the coaching of Jacques Fouroux. Philippe Sella, who won 111 caps at centre, hooker Daniel Dubroca and the peerless full-back Serge Blanco were the mainstays of the side with Blanco proving himself one of the most exciting runners the game has ever seen.

Blanco scored perhaps the most dramatic try of all time to earn France a place in the 1987 World Cup final. Playing Australia in Sydney in the semi-final, the French were behind three times in the match but still snatched an incredible win. David Campese

league players by Scotland in 1953, and they were not accepted as official members of the International Board until 1978.

The French shared the championship in 1954 and 1955 before winning the tournament outright in 1959, 1961 and 1962. From 1961 to 1963, the top scorer in the competition was the French full-back-turned-fly-half Pierre Albaladejo – arguably the first superstar of the Gallic game. Albaladejo was the first Frenchman to land three drop goals in an international when he scored a hat-trick in the 23-6 win over Ireland in 1960. He was given the nickname "Monsieur Drop" and named at fly-half and David Codey scored for Australia and Michael Lynagh's boot kept the favourites in front. Alain Lorieux, Sella and Patrice Lagisquet all crossed for tries but the Aussies led 24-21 as injury time approached. Didier Camberabero levelled the scores with a penalty before Blanco intervened.

From deep in their own half, France ran the ball through 11 pairs of hands before Blanco charged at the line and scored in the corner to silence the Australian crowd. They could not repeat the magic in the final and lost to the All Blacks. The next two World Cups were disappointing and in 1999 they were runners-up again after their magical afternoon at Twickenham against New Zealand in the semi-final.

In Europe, the French were vying

▼ Imanol Harinordoquy of France dominates in the line-out during the Six Nations match against Scotland, 2007.

FRANCE

▲ Former captain
Rafael Ibanez with
the Six Nations
trophy.

the tournament going into the semi-final against England and were strongly fancied to see off Clive Woodward's side who had spluttered in getting the better of Samoa and Wales in particular. As they made the journey to Sydney's Telstra Stadium, the heavens opened and all the French confidence and swagger disappeared as the rain fell.

Fly-half Frederic Michalak was overshadowed by his opposite number Jonny Wilkinson as England's forwards played the conditions perfectly and the Woodward's men ran out comfortable winners.

France and Laporte got their revenge at the first time of asking in the 2004 Six Nations when they rounded off a Grand Slam by beating England in Paris. This was followed by a championship win in 2006 and successful defence in 2007.

France hosted the 2007 World Cup but lost out to England in the semi-finals losing 14-9. They subsequently lost to Argentina in the bronze final to finish the tournament fourth.

Whilst Les Bleus had an indifferent 2008 Six Nations' campaign the argument persists that on their day they are still the best side in Europe.

with England for "top dog" status and won back-to-back Grand Slams in 1997 and 1998. After the 1999 World Cup, coach Jean-Claude Skrela was replaced by Bernard Laporte who took them to a Slam in 2002 but their 2003 World Cup campaign ended in disappointment.

The French were the form team of

Grounds

Rugby union is blessed with so many magnificent stadiums, some the most impressive in their respective countries. The ground that sets the benchmark in the game is the home of English rugby, **Twickenham**.

The Twickenham Stadium – which also housed home games of the Harlequins – made its debut in 1909 when the Quins took on local rivals Richmond, and won 14–10.

A year later the England team ended their nomadic existence and were running out at Twickenham, to beat Wales 11–6, in a season when

▼ The magnificent Twickenham Stadium.

Millennium Stadium.

Built in 1999 for the Rugby World Cup, the Millennium Stadium was constructed on the site of one of the most famous sports venues in the world – the National Stadium, at Cardiff Arms Park.

The Millennium Stadium was a magnificent backdrop to the 1999 World Cup and provided a sensational venue for the final between Australia and France.

▲ The Millennium Stadium hosting the opening ceremony of the 1999 Rugby World Cup.

▶ Murrayfield, home of Scotland.

they won the championship.

To establish the new home of English rugby RFU treasurer, William Cail, paid £5,573 for a cabbage field at Twickenham, which had been discovered by a committee member, Billy Williams.

Now that same cabbage patch has been transformed again into a stadium with a wraparound roof, 83,000 seats, an in-house hotel, health club and leisure centre – even though its location in the midst of a suburban housing estate is far from ideal.

If Twickenham sets the world benchmark there is one ground, across the Severn Bridge, which is a great pretender to their crown, the

Crowds of around 70,000 regularly pack into Twickenham and the Millennium Stadium, especially for Six Nations games but the ground that still holds the record for the championship is Scotland's **Murrayfield**.

Scotland may not have fared well on the pitch in the 1950s but they did break one record. More than 80,000 people came to Murrayfield (a world record for a rugby match at the time) to watch the Scots hammer Wales 19-0 in 1951. Swelling the crowd, and to show that some things never change, there were 25,000 Welshmen in the ground!

Not content with that, and although Scotland failed to win a championship outright during the 1970s, they did play their part in one world record. On St David's Day 1975, 104,000 people flooded into Murrayfield to see the Scots beat Wales 12-10.

Twickenham, the Millennium Stadium and Murrayfield are modern all-seater stadiums but the old ground in Dublin's **Lansdowne Road** was often considered to have the most character and best atmosphere.

The world's oldest rugby ground was opened in 1878, hosting its first international in the same year, against England but has been closed since 2006 for renovation (re-opening is planned for April 2010) while Irish rugby games have been played at the magnificent new 82,500-seat stadium Croke Park.

France also have one of the newest stadiums in the rugby world, in the 80,000-seat **Stade de France**. Built for the 1998 Football World Cup it has developed into one of the most atmospheric grounds in the world and

▲ The atmospheric Lansdowne Road.

▲ The magnificent Stade de France hosting the 2007 World Cup final.

▲▲ Eden Park, Auckland, hosting a Super 12 game.

hosted the 2007 Rugby World Cup final won by South Africa.

Stadium Australia, opened in 1999, also hosted a World Cup final in 2003. The site of a former abattoir, 10 miles west of Sydney, it set the world record for attendance at a rugby match when 108,878 came to see New Zealand against Australia, in 2000.

Stadium Australia isn't the only stunning stadium in the southern hemisphere and although those in neighbouring New Zealand aren't as big, their names are steeped in the very history of rugby.

Eden Park in Auckland is perhaps the most famous in the land of the long white cloud.

It has been in existence as a sports ground since the year 1900. It became the home of Auckland Cricket in 1910 and the home of Auckland Rugby in 1925 after the Union had leased the grounds since 1914.

Eden Park, which is a very open arena and unlike most others in the rugby world, hosted the first World Cup final, in 1987. It has been used for Test rugby in 1921. Its current capacity for rugby is 45,472 and 42,000 for cricket.

On New Zealand's south island the Test venue in Dunedin is the famous **Carisbrook** ground. The 33,000 capacity home to the Otago Highlanders Carisbrook was transferred

▲ Ellis Park,
Johannesburg.

to the Otago Rugby Football Union in June 1907 and, in 1981, the ORFU bought the freehold land title from the Presbyterian Church.

In South Africa there are some sensational rugby stadiums but one stands out above all others, the scene of the 1995 World Cup final – **Ellis Park**.

First opened in 1928 after the Transvaal rugby union negotiated for the site with a Mr JD Ellis the ground has become synonymous with South African rugby.

The stadium, which now holds 80,000, was redeveloped at a cost of £60 million. The new Ellis Park rose in 1982, the bill boosted by many problems along the way.

Ellis Park was also the scene when South Africa re-entered international rugby in 1992 with a Test match against New Zealand.

Today Ellis Park is the home ground of the Lions, the Cats, Kaizer Chiefs Football Club and is also the premier concert event in South Africa.

Eden Park, Carisbrook and Ellis Park have been the scene of a number of sensational 15-a-side encounters but for classic Sevens there's only one place to go, the **Hong Kong Stadium**.

The ground may not be the biggest in the world, holding 40,000 people, but it has been important in the development of the game, bringing it to new audiences.

In the So Kon Po valley this impressive stadium was built in 1994, a gift from the Hong Kong Jockey Club to the island.

Heineken Cup

▶ Toulouse and Cardiff played out the first ever Heineken European Cup final in 1996.

One of the biggest successes of professional rugby in the Northern Hemisphere, the Heineken (European) Cup was launched in 1995. It was started under the initiative of the then Five Nations Committee who were looking for a new level of cross–border competition to bridge the gap between a country's domestic league and international matches.

The Super 10 (and then Super 12) was the forerunner of the Heineken Cup in the southern hemisphere. Whilst the Super 12 received universal acceptance from the off, the Heineken Cup kicked off with 12 teams from Ireland, France, Wales, Italy and Romania, with Scotland and England absent.

The first match took place in Romania with Farul Constanta losing to the eventual first champions Toulouse, 10-35. The English and Scottish sides didn't stay out in the cold for long, and a year later the revamped Heineken Cup kicked off with 20 teams in four pools.

The main difference between the Super 12 and the Heineken is the composition of teams.

All the sides in the Super 12 represent provinces while in the Heineken Cup there is a mixture of provinces, club and district sides. The Irish teams represent their provinces,

▲ Brive
captain Alain
Penaud holds
the Heineken
European cup
after beating
Leicester in the
1997 final.

like Munster, Leinster and Ulster, while
in England it is club sides like Leicester,
Bath and Northampton that take part.

The diversity of the sides and the
history that accompanies so many
of them brings a breadth and tradition
to the competition that no other
can match.

Before those giants of the English
game arrived Toulouse emerged as the
first champions, winning a final 21-18
at the National Stadium in Wales,
against Cardiff.

Without the English sides the
first tournament failed to capture the
imagination of the European rugby
public and just 21,800 spectators
watched that first final. Although from
then on the tournament grew and grew.

Any doubts about the future of
the tournament were ended in the
following season. The resolve of the
organising committee was proved
correct with Scottish and English sides
confirming the Heineken Cup as a truly
pan-European tournament, already
bridging the gap between domestic and
international rugby.

The arrival of the English and
Scottish teams in the 1996-97 season,
meant the Cup now embraced 20
teams, the four pools were fiercely
competitive. Only Leicester and Brive
emerged from the pool stages unbeaten.

▲ Jubilant Bath fans after their victory in 1998.

Giants like Wasps, Leinster and Munster failed to make the quarter-finals.

Three English sides made the last eight with Leicester moving into the final, where they faced Brive in front of 41,664 fans, again at the National Stadium in Wales. Significantly the final was watched by almost double the number of supporters as 12 months earlier. A live TV audience also brought the final to 35 million viewers in 86 countries. The Heineken Cup had arrived with a bang!

The 1997 final failed to go Leicester's way, Brive winning 28-9.

The 1998 final will go down in history as one of the most dramatic, Bath and their travelling army of supporters beating holders Brive at a packed Stade Lescure Stadium in Bordeaux, 19-18.

"That was a day of drama and no little emotion, especially for an ex-Bath man" recalled Sky Sports commentator and former England outside-half Stuart Barnes.

"We left the ground and knew a great sporting tournament was up and running. Few would argue that rugby union has found itself a special as the best of Europe crosses borders to provide action, atmosphere, the whole panacea."

A row between Heineken Cup organisers, ERC, and the English clubs led to a boycott by the latter of the 1998-99 tournament. This ensured that Bath were unable to defend the crown they won, the 16 remaining teams taking part in four pools of four.

Many felt the absence of the English sides would lead to a French domination but it was an Irish side, Ulster that upset the odds to win it.

French clubs filled the top spot in three of the groups. But Ulster beat Toulouse (twice) and reigning French champions Stade Francais on their way to a Dublin final against Colomiers, who they beat 21-6.

A capacity Lansdowne Road crowd of 49,000 watched Ulster win, along with a worldwide television audience estimated at over 36 million.

The new decade saw the start of an English domination of the Heineken Cup with the first three finals of the new Millennium being won by top English sides.

The 1999-2000 tournament set a new record when for the first time four different nations – England, Ireland, France and Wales – made it through to the semi-finals.

But it was the English side (Northampton) and the Irish (Munster) who turned up at Twickenham in front of a record crowd of 68,441, as Northampton won 9-8.

Once one Midlands side had won it, it was left to another one, Leicester, to take a firm grip on the trophy. The Tigers became the first side to win it twice and they managed it in back-to-back years.

The losing finalists of 1997, Leicester, took their first Heineken Cup in 2001, beating Stade Francais in their home town of Paris, in a sensational final, 34-30.

More sold out signs went up for this final, Leicester outscoring the Paris club three tries to none. Centre Leon Lloyd scored two and flanker Neil Back one so they could walk off with the massive trophy.

◄ Simon Mason of Ulster kicks for goal against Colomiers 1999.

▼ Jubilant Toulouse fans after their victory in 2005.

▲ Munster players celebrate with the trophy following victory over Toulouse, 2008.

Leicester's second title came in Cardiff, in 2002, when they beat Munster in front of a tournament record 74,000 crowd, 15-9. Tries from Geordan Murphy and Austin Healey and the illegal intervention of Neil Back at a scrum, knocking the ball out of Munster scrum-half Peter Stringer's hand, taking Leicester home.

The eighth Heineken Cup final, in 2003, broke more new ground, as it was the first all-French affair; Toulouse beating Perpignan 22-17.

The French domination was broken, a year later in 2004, when Wasps, fittingly at Twickenham, won a thrilling final against the holders;

Rob Howley, snatching a last-minute try to give his side the win, 27-20. Howley swooped on a bouncing ball to touch down under the nose of Toulouse full-back Clément Poitrenaud, in front of 73,057 fans.

The 10th anniversary final saw Toulouse beat Stade Francais 18-12 while Munster claimed an epic title, with a 23-19 victory at the Millennium Stadium in 2006.

Munster have subsequently won the competition again (with Wasps sandwiched in between their victories in 2007) and are now challenging Toulouse as the tournament's most successful team.

Ireland

With sports like Gaelic football, hurling and soccer taking so much of the attention in Ireland the rugby union side has one of the smallest player bases amongst the major unions. Compared to England's 200,000 players Ireland have just 11,500, across 200 clubs. That hasn't stopped them pulling off some sensational results against the world's top teams.

The game originated in Ireland around 1850, probably started by former pupils of Rugby School and Cheltenham College, who played the game at Trinity College, Dublin.

Ireland played their first international, against England, in 1875 at Kennington Oval and this was the beginning of a tough opening period for the Irish. After losing that first game to England, comprehensively, they had to wait six years for their first win, a

▲ Gordon D'Arcy, player of the tournament in the 2004 Six Nations.

victory over Scotland.

That first international side had nine from Dublin University and six from the North of Ireland, demonstrating a unique mixture.

Today the national side is almost exclusively made up of players from their four provinces Munster, Leinster, Ulster and Connacht, three from the south and one from the north of Ireland.

Throughout history, despite the political troubles between the north and the south, the Ireland rugby team has always been selected from players from both sides of the border.

Irish politics did affect rugby in the

▲ Irish Grand Slam hero Jackie Kyle.

1970s, with the 1972 season becoming a non-event in championship terms. Due to the troubles in Ireland both of their home games were cancelled and Wales, playing three games only ended unbeaten and on top of the table. Ireland with only two games to their name were also unbeaten.

Unbeaten runs for Ireland were rare in the early years. Although they did pick up Triple Crowns (victories over England, Wales and Scotland in one season) in 1894 and 1899 their overall record in the championship is worse than any other of the sides, bar Italy.

England, Scotland and Wales all won Grand Slams (victories over all the other nations in one season) in the early years of the Five Nations but Ireland had to wait until after the Second World War for their first clean sweep.

Despite having some great teams in the last century, the Irish side have only managed to deliver one Grand Slam to their long-suffering fans, in 1948.

The Irish road to the Grand Slam had begun a year earlier with the first Five Nations championship since the War. The title was shared between Wales and England but already the Irish were starting to

show the green shoots of recovery and to build a formidable side.

A capacity 32,000 crowd packed into Ravenhill to see Ireland clinch their first Grand Slam with a 6-3 victory over Wales. Outside-half Jackie Kyle and hooker Karl Mullen were two of their greatest heroes. This Ireland side scored 10 tries in their four games, a better record than for the 20 years before.

Crucially Ireland had built a magnificent back-row for that Grand Slam year in Des O'Brien, Bill McKay and Jim McCarthy. Kyle – the genius at fly-half – was for many people one of the greatest players ever to play rugby union.

A Triple Crown followed Ireland's 1948 Grand Slam, a year later, but they had to wait until the 1970s and 1980s for more glory.

Ireland won the championship in 1974, and they had Mike Gibson – who scored two tries against England – ruling the roost in the backs. They also had a certain legend, called Willie John McBride in the pack. (See M for McBride).

Twenty one points from Ollie Campbell for Ireland against Scotland at Lansdowne Road delivered a rare

◀ Ireland scrum-half John Moloney races clear to score a crucial try in Ireland's 26-21 victory over England at Twickenham, 1974.

Triple Crown in 1982. Three years later the Irish came closer still to the Five Nations' ultimate prize. This time they were thwarted by a bruising 15-15 draw with the French, in Dublin, but they still ended the season one point clear at the top.

Again the Irish looked to the boot, but this time it belonged to Michael Kiernan, who slotted five penalties from seven attempts, while the French scored two tries.

Ireland won the 1985 Triple Crown and the championship in a 13-10

Dublin win over England. Again it was Kiernan who proved the hero dropping

◀ Michael Kiernan, so often the kicking hero for Ireland.

▶ Captain Brian O'Driscoll with the Triple Crown trophy celebrates with his team-mates.

a vital, injury time goal.

Nineteen long years passed until Ireland pulled off their next, remarkable Triple Crown, and second place in the championship, in 2004.

In 2006, Ireland showed the capacity to play top class rugby, but only inconsistently – a rout of Wales was balanced by uncertain victories against England, Scotland and Italy and a comprehensive defeat by winners France. Ireland finished second and won the Triple Crown for the second time in three years, incidentally the first ever time a trophy had been awarded for the feat.

After disappointing World Cup and Six Nations campaigns, Eddie O'Sullivan resigned as Ireland coach in March 2008, to be replaced by Declan Kidney following on from his successful tenure as head coach of Munster.

Johnno, Jason and Jonny

▲ The England 2003 World Cup squad.

Clive Woodward knew in his heart of hearts that his England side that won the World Cup would never play again and his feelings were confirmed when captain and king of the rugby jungle Martin Johnson retired from international rugby prior to the 2004 Six Nations. The 114-times capped prop Jason Leonard won his final cap against Italy in that competition whilst Jonny Wilkinson was ruled out of the tournament with a neck injury.

Wilkinson has returned to continue his assault on the record books, but Johnson and Leonard are gone forever from the international stage. Will we see

their like again? It is doubtful. When Leonard bowed out, the trio had won precisely 250 caps between them and scored 832 points of which Wilkinson had contributed 817.

The older pair were the last of a dying breed in that they had actually tasted real life before becoming full time rugby players when the game went professional in 1995. Leonard worked as a carpenter, once returning to his building site the day after an international to make up time lost at training, and Johnson was probably the world's most unlikely bank clerk. The thought of asking Johnson for a loan probably never crossed the minds of his opponents over the years who he gave precisely nothing bar a handshake once the game was over.

JOHNNO, JASON AND JONNY

▲ Martin Johnson in action in the 2003 World Cup. England's greatest ever player?

▼ "How Much Longer?!" Jason Leonard looks up to the Gods in 2000.

Johnson can legitimately lay claim to being the greatest player England has ever produced although he wouldn't do it himself. The records support this assertion; Three Lions tours, including two as captain, two Grand Slams, a World Cup, four Zurich Premierships, back-to-back Heineken Cups, 84 caps and two international tries.

He is the first to admit that his playing style was hardened by a stint in New Zealand as a teenager and no less a judge than Colin Meads wanted him as an All Black. But he made his England debut against France in 1993. He was flown out as a Lions replacement later in the year, went virtually straight into the Test team and was a first choice for England ever since.

Johnson won his first Grand Slam under Will Carling in 1995 and led the Lions to victory over South Africa in 1997. He was not national captain at the time but as manager Fran Cotton said; "We wanted someone who would knock on the opposition dressing room and intimidate them." He managed that, but his game was not just built on his undoubted hardness and he turned himself into the archetypal, all-purpose, multi-tasking modern lock in the last six years of his career. He was the best forward at the 2003 World Cup having tacked running and handling skills on to the historical basics of second-row play. He became England captain in 1999 and his men would follow him anywhere. It is now hoped that his inspirational leadership will once again bring success to the national team following his appointment as head coach in April 2008.

Leonard was in the trenches with Johnson for most of his international career which began in the intensely hostile environs of Buenos Aires in 1990. There are still English pressmen wandering around patting themselves on the back for predicting that the Barking lad would win a century of caps and 13 years later they were proved right when Leonard led the England team out against France. One press box veteran recalls that after the first scrum against the fearsome Argentinean pack in Leonard's debut international, he turned to a colleague and said "We've got one here". England certainly did have one and Leonard overtook Philippe Sella as the world's most capped player when he came on as a replacement against France in the 2003 World Cup semi-final.

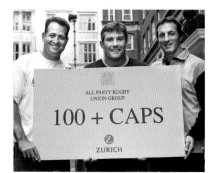

◄ Rugby's three
centurions – David
Campese (left)
Jason Leonard
and Philippe Sella
(right).

To put his achievements into perspective, consider that Sella was a centre and rugby's other centurion, David Campese, was a winger. Leonard was a prop, could play equally well on either side of the scrum and underwent a career-threatening neck operation in 1992.

Leonard's versatility served him well as did his ability to adapt to the professional era. He is one of rugby's most sociable players and always sought out his opposite number for a pint after a game. But you don't get to 100 caps by being in the bar all the time and Leonard knew there was a time and a place for everything.

Whilst Leonard and Johnson would not win any prizes in a beauty contest, Wilkinson had become the darling of the media even before dropping the goal that won the World Cup. Only Will

Carling has enjoyed, or in Wilkinson's case endured, such a high profile, but he takes it all in his stride and refuses to let the demands of the insatiable British press impinge on the most important thing in his life, namely rugby.

Wilkinson was first capped as an 18-year-old replacement against Ireland in 1998 and has hardly been out of the team since. His first start in an England shirt did not go totally to plan as he was on the wrong end of a 76-0 beating from Australia in Brisbane on the famous "Tour of Hell" in June 1998.

In the following year's World Cup, Northampton's Paul Grayson was preferred as England went out to South Africa in the quarter-finals in Paris, but Wilkinson was back in the side for the 2000 Six Nations and the subsequent summer tour when he masterminded a second Test victory over the Springboks which triggered England's period of domination over the Southern Hemisphere's Big Three.

After helping England secure the Grand Slam in 2003, Wilkinson was the subject of intense scrutiny at that year's World Cup, not least by the Australian press who were clearly running scared of England's peerless match winner.

▲ Jonny Wilkinson celebrating scoring 1000 test points in his career.

His immaculate goal-kicking kept England in the tournament when they were misfiring and saw off the French in the semi-final. Inevitably, it was a Wilkinson drop goal that won the cup, his kick sparking celebrations not seen in England since the triumph in that other World Cup in 1966.

Due to a non-contact ankle injury sustained in training, Wilkinson was not included in the teams for the opening games of the World Cup 2007 against the United States and South Africa. He returned to score 24 points in the 44-22 win over Samoa and helped England to their victory against Tonga which put them through to the quarter-finals. During England's 12-10 quarter-final win against Australia, in which he scored all of England's points, Wilkinson became the Rugby World Cup's leading point-scorer with 231 points, surpassing Gavin Hastings of Scotland. He continued to play a major role in England's defence of the World Cup by kicking nine points, including a last gasp 40-metre drop goal, in their 14-9 semi-final victory over France. In the final, South Africa emerged victorious although Wilkinson still slotted home two penalties but showed his fallibility by missing two drop kick attempts.

A litany of injuries – to his knee ligaments, arm, shoulder and kidney – meant that he did not appear again for England after the World Cup until the opening game of the 2007 Six Nations championship against Scotland in which he scored 27 points in the game (a record in the Calcutta Cup) and was awarded Man of the Match. The following week against Italy, he became the highest point-scorer in the history of the Five/Six Nations championship.

In the 2008 Six Nations, in the match against Italy, he became the first English player to score 1000 Test points. He is also the world record drop goal scorer in international rugby with a total of 29. In March 2008, he became international rugby's record point-scorer of all time, overtaking Neil Jenkins of Wales.

If he had kept clear of injury, who knows what he could have achieved!

Kickers

Throughout rugby's history there are countless examples of when the boot was mightier than the sword. Kicks have been winning games since the days when William Webb Ellis was supposed to have picked up the ball. Two World Cup finals have been decided by late drop goals so the role of the kicker can never be over-estimated and every great team has had a player who is deadly with the boot. In this chapter we look at four of the most successful goal-kickers in the history of the game.

1. NEIL JENKINS
Wales/Lions – Test points: 1090
If you had to place your last penny on a man to kick a penalty you wouldn't go far wrong with the man they called the "Ginger Monster", Neil Jenkins.

The outside-half from Church Village ended his career with an incredible 1049 points for Wales (41 for the Lions) to his name, from 87 Tests, more than 200 better

▲ The most famous kick in the history of rugby!

◀ Neil Jenkins in 2001, the year he surpassed 1000 points in Test matches.

▶ Diego
Dominguez
playing for Stade
Francais.

than his nearest rival.

His record is all the more remarkable if you consider he played for a Wales team that struggled in the 1990s and he was subjected to comparisons with the legendary No 10s who he followed into the famous red shirt.

There's no question that Jenkins outlasted all his critics and became, in 2001, the first player to score 1000 points in Test matches.

"Whatever figures I end with will be overtaken at some time in the future, but the first player to reach 1,000 points holds that honour for eternity," said Jenkins.

He made his Wales debut in 1991 but for many rugby fans it will be his role in the 2001 Lions series win over South Africa where he is most fondly remembered.

Those Lions won a Test series in South Africa for the first time in 23 years and it was the ice cool kicking of Jenkins that regularly kept them on track.

The end of Jenkins' international career certainly wasn't the end of his goal-kicking feats. In 2004, playing for the Celtic Warriors he converted a remarkable 44 consecutive kicks.

2. DIEGO DOMINGUEZ
Italy/Argentina – Test points: 1010

When Italy were admitted to the Six Nations in 2000 it was in no small part to the influence of Diego Dominguez.

The Argentinean born fly-half made his debut in 1991 against France and from then until his final game in 2003 many of Italy's best performances revolved around him.

It is one thing to be kicking goals from every corner of the field when your side is winning, when your pack is on top and the pressure is not at its highest. So in many ways, with Italy often on the back foot, the kicking record of Dominguez stands the test of time even more impressively than some of his rivals.

Dominguez changed allegiance to Italy after waiting behind Hugo Porta, in Argentina, for his chance in international rugby. A season in France and then another in Italy convinced him to move to the Azzurri, qualifying through his grandmother.

Dominguez was the lynchpin of three Italian World Cup campaigns, playing in the 1991, 1995 and 1999 tournaments.

His influence on the Italian team was best demonstrated by the reaction to his first retirement from international rugby in 2000. He was coaxed back by then coach Brad Johnstone and the hopes of the Italian nation, eventually giving way before the 2003 World Cup after 74 caps.

Dominguez played for the French club Stade Francais between 1997 and 2004, helping them to the domestic championship in 1998.

3. ANDREW MEHRTENS
New Zealand – Test points: 967
One of the finest outside-halves of his generation Andrew Mehrtens is the most prolific goal-kicker in the history of New Zealand rugby.

Mehrtens made his All Blacks debut in 1995, playing in the World Cup final later in that season.

He overtook Grant Fox as the highest point-scorer in New Zealand Test history in 2000.

No one has scored more penalties (181), drop goals (10) or conversions (162) than Mehrtens, who is also New Zealand's most capped outside-half. Mehrtens is the leading scorer in the Tri Nations, with 309 points in the annual competition.

A proud Canterbury Crusader, Mehrtens was an integral part of their incredible run of three consecutive Super 12 titles, which started in 1998.

▼ Andrew Mehrtens lines up another for the All Blacks.

▼ Michael Lynagh burst onto the scene in Australia's 1984 Grand Slam tour.

Mehrtens toured Europe with the All Blacks in 2002 but was one of the high profile absentees from John Mitchell's 2003 World Cup squad. However the All Blacks failed to find a dependable goal-kicker to take his place and significantly he signed a new one-year contract with the New Zealand Rugby Union in 2003.

4. MICHAEL LYNAGH
Australia – Test points: 911

When Neil Jenkins went to the top of the international kicking league in 1999 it was by overtaking the record of the remarkable Michael Lynagh.

The Queensland outside-half was part of the sensational Australian side of the mid-1980s that went on to lift the Rugby World Cup, at Twickenham in 1991.

Lynagh made his debut for Australia in 1984 announcing his abilities to the world on the Wallabies' Grand Slam tour of Britain and Ireland later that year.

The Australians were desperate for a man to fill the boots of the legendary Mark Ella and in Lynagh – who played centre in 1984 – they found a player that was more than up to the task.

Lynagh overtook Andy Irvine as the world's leading scorer at the 1987 World Cup, accumulating 72 caps and 911 points in his career, captaining the Wallabies 15 times.

Goal-kicking wasn't the only area in which Lynagh broke records. Lynagh at No 10 and Nick Farr-Jones at No 9 lined-up together for the Wallabies, 47 times between 1985 and 1992, more than any other half-backs in the history of the game.

England's win over Australia in the quarter-finals of the 1995 World Cup was Lynagh's last Test. Once he'd quit the international scene he moved to England to play for Saracens, before becoming a television pundit.

Lynagh's Wallaby coach Bob Dwyer said of him; "Michael is very controlled as a person and possesses tremendous composure. I cannot remember an occasion when I saw him panic. As a player he also had tremendous running skills and width of vision, not to mention his obvious kicking ability."

Lions

The Lions represent the enduring fascination of rugby. They are fact for a while and then they become legends. There is no other side like them in the world because they compete at the very pinnacle of the game for a short, breathless time, and are then consigned to history.

It has always been like that. The Lions started life as the British Isles Rugby Union Tourists back in 1924 and, although they are more accurately described these days as the British and Irish Lions, the pattern of their operation is unchanged.

They now play major Test series, with other supporting games, in Australia, New Zealand and South Africa every four years. The squad is put together, meets its commitments and then breaks up.

The tours these days are extremely

▲ Dr Ronald Cove-Smith with the ship's captain en route to Cape Town with the 1924 Lions.

demanding. Once, the Lions would play 25 games or so on the road but in response to today's demands on players they face no more than a dozen matches, including three Tests, on their ventures. "I went to South Africa with the '55 Lions and we were there for

▲ Welsh legend Cliff Morgan during the 1955 Lions series against South Africa.

wherever they are. "When I went on the 1938 tour to South Africa there were no journalists from home with us," said the late Vivian Jenkins, the former Wales full-back.

It was obvious from the start of the Lions' existence that winning a Test series anywhere in the Southern Hemisphere was a demanding business. That made it all the more rewarding when they claimed even a single Test victory – they took one in New Zealand in 1930 and another in South Africa in 1938.

After the Second World War, the Lions did not return to business until 1950 with a 23-match tour of New Zealand. Next, the legend of the Lions acquired another significant chapter in 1955 when they shared the Test series with South Africa 2-2 and established all kinds of records, including a crowd of 95,000 for the first Test in Johannesburg. The Lions won that Test 23-22 with the South African Jack van der Schyff just failing to kick a goal in the last minute for victory.

The 1955 Lions woke up the world of rugby. They had set new benchmarks for the British and Irish game and everyone wanted more. All this fuelled

four months," remembers the great Welsh fly-half Cliff Morgan. "We had time to take in so much around the tour as well as play the matches."

Modern communications have brought the Lions into the homes of their key fans thousands of miles away. In 1974, for example, when the Lions won a Test series in South Africa for the first time, TV viewers in Britain did not see the action until three days later. Now, all Lions' games are televised live massive expectation for the 1959 tour to Australia and New Zealand (Australia had to wait another 30 years for the Lions to tour there exclusively).

Ronnie Dawson, the Ireland hooker, was tour captain and after the Lions had swept through Australia unbeaten, winning two Tests, New Zealand could not wait for them. More than 800,000 watched the 25 games played there. But there was scant reward for the Lions in international terms and their first Test defeat by 18-17, six penalties against four tries, is a bitter memory to this day. New Zealand won the first three Tests, the Lions the last.

Three more Lions' tours in the 1960s, two to South Africa, one to

Australia and New Zealand, saw the Southern Hemisphere remain on top, but the 1970s brought dramatic changes, beginning with the tour to Australia and New Zealand in 1971. The Lions knew they had an outstanding squad under the captaincy of the Welsh centre John Dawes, with another Welshman, Carwyn James, in charge of coaching.

But what made this tour stand out so strongly in the eyes of the world was the Welsh half-back pairing of Gareth Edwards and Barry John whose work behind a well-organised pack of forwards was mercurial. Edwards could

◀ Ronnie Dawson, captain of the 1959 Lions Tour.

▼ "The King" Barry John was imperious during the 1971 tour of New Zealand.

▲ Willie John McBride leads out Gareth Edwards and the rest of the 1974 Lions.

The next mission, to South Africa, was only three years later and this time the captaincy was in the hands of the Ulsterman Willie John McBride, on his fifth Lions tour and very determined to take the battle to the very heart of the Springboks' strength – their powerful and match-hardened forwards. Again, the Lions depended on a hard core of 17 players who played in all four Tests and throughout the 22-match trip the Lions remained unbeaten.

The Lions rampaged through South African rugby, setting and raising standards match by match under McBride's cold-eyed leadership. They took the first Test 12-3, the second 28-9 and the series clincher at Port Elizabeth by 26-9. It was then something of an anticlimax when they were held to a draw in the final Test.

From this high point, the Lions were to fall behind once more. They lost in New Zealand in 1977, in South Africa in 1980 and in New Zealand again in 1983. And with the first Rugby World Cup to be played in 1987, there were some doubts whether the Lions would survive in the changing structure of the game.

But in 1989, on their first tour

play for only 10 minutes in the first Test but John was in full command throughout and kicked two penalties as the Lions won 9-3.

New Zealand stormed back in the second Test, winning 22-12, but there was more than enough belief in the Lions' camp that they could take the series and they went on to do so with a 13-3 win in the third Test and a 14-14 draw in the last. John, who was one of 12 players to appear in all four Tests, scored 191 points in 17 matches and was given the nickname "King" during the tour.

solely to Australia, the Lions, led by the Scottish back-row forward Finlay Calder, brought their cause right back to the top of the agenda. Against an Australian squad, the bulk of whom were to capture the World Cup two years later, Calder and his men overturned defeat in the first Test to take the next two for the series, finishing in style in Sydney where they punished a glaring error by David Campese, the brilliant but opinionated Australian wing.

Four years later, under another Scot, Gavin Hastings, the Lions lost the series 2-1 in New Zealand. In 1997, with England's Martin Johnson at the helm, they stunned the South Africans by winning the most recent series there 2-1, winning the first two Tests to emphasise their strengths.

Thus, it was no surprise that the 2001 Lions under Johnson went to Australia as narrow favourites, followed by thousands of optimistic, red-shirted fans. That series was destined to go down to the wire and the Lions, after winning the opening Test in fine style, suffered the ultimate disappointment of losing the next two, the last by a margin of 29-23.

The Lions then went, in the space of four years from losing on a knife-edge to enduring the biggest hammering in their history, in New Zealand, in 2005.

They were not just beaten by the All Blacks, but humiliated under the coaching of Sir Clive Woodward. All three Tests were lost, the second Test 48-18, although in mitigation they lost Lawrence Dallaglio, captain Brian O'Driscoll and key man Richard Hill, to injury. Dallaglio went in the first game and the other two within 18 minutes of the start of the first Test.

The Lions will tour current world champions South Africa in 2009, with Ian McGeechan as their coach and HSBC as their shirt-sponsor.

▼ Ian McGeechan who will be the coach for the 2009 British and Irish Lions tour to South Africa.

McBride and Meads

Willie John Mcbride and Colin Meads were born a world apart, McBride in Northern Ireland and Meads in the North Island of New Zealand. Yet because of rugby, these two icons of the game became the closest of rivals, the greatest of friends.

In his 55 Test matches for New Zealand, right in the heart of the All Blacks pack, Meads reckoned he played against McBride more times than any other opponent and regarded him as the greatest of competitors. According to Meads, they had "some rare old contests" and he respected McBride for his tenacity and his ability, adding that few packs would have had a more devoted and fired-up core man.

On opposite sides, Meads for New Zealand and McBride for the British and Irish Lions, their rivalry reached a peak in the 1971 Test series in New Zealand – which the Lions won. McBride still recalls putting his arm around Meads at the end of the final Test and thinking; "This is what I had dreamed of, beating the All Blacks on their own soil."

These two men came from totally different backgrounds but grew up record five tours with the British and Irish Lions, played in 17 Tests, and was captain of the unbeaten 1974 squad in South Africa. Ireland won the Five Nations' championship in 1974 under McBride's leadership.

Both men are of farming stock. McBride was one of six children, born in County Antrim. His father died when he was aged four and the family was brought up by his mother on a small farm. McBride's only club, from start to finish, was Ballymena and it was from their second-row that he graduated to the Ireland side in 1962, winning his first cap against England.

He and two other great Irish players, full-back Tom Kiernan and centre Mike Gibson, were to be the backbone of the team for a decade.

McBride's farewell game in Dublin was in 1975 when he led a joint Ireland-Scotland team to victory over England-Wales in the Ireland centenary match by 17-10. At the start of the following season, he told the Ulster team that he no longer wished to be considered for them – and by definition his Ireland days were over as well. Eight years later, he coached Ireland for a season when the side failed to win a game.

◄ Willie John McBride (left) and Colin Meads (right). Similar players.

to dominate rugby at the highest level. Meads played 55 Tests for New Zealand between 1957 and 1971 while McBride played 63 Tests for Ireland between 1962 and 1975, 43 of them in succession which overtook the record set previously by the Scotland prop Hugh McLeod.

To underscore the statistical difference between the two men a little further, McBride made a

▲ Willie John McBride takes on England in 1974, Ireland's championship-winning year.

Much as McBride was born, shaped and driven by Irish rugby at all of its levels, it was unquestionably in the red shirt of the Lions that he made his greatest impact on the world stage. There was no World Cup in those days, and meetings between the leading nations of the world were far fewer. As a result, tours by the Lions were eagerly awaited and played out before massive crowds.

In 1986, at Cardiff, the Lions made a rare appearance at home to play the rest of the world in a match to mark the centenary of the International Rugby Board. "It has always been my view that there is no greater honour for any sportsman than to represent his country," McBride said at the time. "To be selected for the Lions and don the famous red jersey was the special icing on a most enjoyable playing career."

When McBride captained the Lions in South Africa in 1974, his players still recall the incredible tension in the squad before they won the decisive third Test. They remember the final team meeting before they left for the ground and some believe not a word was said. McBride just looked each player in the eyes and then asked simply; "Men, are we ready?"

Colin Meads, the rangy hill-country farmer, was called Pine Tree from an early age. He was not a world figure in the way that many players are these days because there was nothing like the same exposure from television and other media for the game. But he was respected everywhere, and certainly feared by many throughout the game, and the longer he played the more his legend grew.

He farmed at the hamlet of Te Kuiti in King Country and he would work all day and then train in the evening for his next game. Meads was born for rugby – he weighed 11lbs at birth, one pound less than his brother Stan. He left school before his 15th birthday to begin his enduring relationship with farming and rugby.

On the other side of the world, Willie John McBride would join a bank in Ballymena, his only job.

Meads began his international career in 1957 against Australia in Sydney. He scored a try in his second match. In eight of his 15 years in the New Zealand side, the team was unbeaten. Match by match, his aura grew. But in 1967, playing against Scotland in Edinburgh, Meads was sent off for lunging at one of his opponents.

He was the first player to be sent off in an international for 42 years and his dismissal brought reactions and debate far beyond a straightforward international rugby match. It consumed New Zealand. One of the biggest names in world rugby had been dismissed and, to this day, there are people who are still prepared to debate the whys and wherefore of the incident.

McBride learned much from Meads, even if their playing contacts were

▲ Colin "Pine Tree" Meads in action against France in 1968.

limited. They were similar players in that neither was a classic line-out stylist. Of course, they could win the ball and win it well. What happened next demonstrated the sheer combativeness of both players.

Indeed the story is told of McBride and Meads in opposition for the first time, Ireland v New Zealand at Lansdowne Road in Dublin in 1963.

▼ Willie John McBride takes on Colin Meads' Wellington during the 1971 Lions Tour.

McBride reminded Meads that he was around and Meads went down. Meads was then told by his captain Wilson Whineray to get up and make the next line-out. He did. Minutes later, McBride was down.

The two great men last competed against each other in Auckland in 1971, Meads as captain of New Zealand, McBride as a key forward for the Lions. That the Lions won that four-Test series is history but Meads has always believed that his team was in something of a dip and that the Lions, shamelessly copying some aspects of New Zealand forward play, knew it and benefited from it.

Meads played on for two more years and bowed out in a match at Wellington where thousands bade him farewell.

McBride's own tribute was; "Colin was the best, most aggressive and, perhaps, the most totally committed player I ever played against."

New Zealand

Since rugby kicked off its international life at the end of the 19th century one side has set the benchmark. One side is feared throughout the rugby world. One side is the team to beat at every Rugby World Cup – the New Zealand All Blacks.

Rugby is the national sport in New Zealand. Everyone – men and women – seems to have played, everyone loves the game and everyone pays attention when the All Blacks are in town.

The first recorded game in New Zealand took place in May 1870; its introduction in the country credited to Charles John Monro.

The first fully representative team was the 1893 team that made the trip to New South Wales, captained by

▲ The All Blacks perform the haka prior to the 2008 Bledisloe Cup match against The Wallabies

Tom Ellison. New Zealand played their first Test match in 1903, a victory over Australia, 22-3. Albert Asher scored their first try and the first points came from Billy Wallace.

Many things characterise the New Zealand All Blacks, setting them apart from most others, and one of those things is the challenge they set down to every team they face, with their haka.

Before every Test match the whole All Blacks side – usually led by a Maori player – take part in the war dance in the centre of the pitch. An event to send chills down the spine.

The first time the haka was seen in

the UK was during the 1888–89 tour. Then a side, made up mainly of Maoris, played an incredible 107 matches in 14 months, on a trip that took in both Australia and the UK.

No history of New Zealand rugby should ignore the debt the All Blacks hold to the Maori. They still have their own international side – but not Test recognised – and they have left an indelible mark on New Zealand, and world rugby.

► George Nepia was one of the stars of the New Zealand "Invincibles" of 1924-25.

In the early years of international rugby two New Zealand sides changed the face of the game.

The first in 1905 was known as The Originals. Captained by the legendary Dave Gallaher his team won all but one of an incredible 33-match tour, scoring 868 points and conceding just 47. The only defeat on the tour coming in controversial circumstances, against Wales, 3-0.

Following Gallaher's side, the

◀ Brian Lochore introduces his 1967 All Blacks to the Queen at Twickenham.

1924-25 All Blacks – The Invincibles – swept all before them beating Ireland 6-0, Wales 19-0 and England 17-11. In the 1920s, All Blacks like Bert Cooke, George Nepia, and Maurice and Cyril Brownlie were seen and never forgotten.

Historically New Zealand's fiercest opponents are South Africa. The Springboks first toured New Zealand in 1921, a drawn 1-1 series setting the tone for decades of hard-fought, colossal

rugby. In that series the last Test was drawn 0-0 and in 1928 when New Zealand went to South Africa again there was nothing to separate the teams. This time they tied the series 2-2.

The All Blacks have produced some of the best rugby in the game's history and in the 1950s they became the undisputed world champions.

In 1949 the All Blacks lost every one of the six Tests in which they played but from 1950 went on an incredible run, losing just five of their 24 internationals.

The 3-0 series victory over the Lions in 1950 started the renaissance and in 1956 New Zealand won a Test series against South Africa for the first time.

This time it was Don Clarke, or Superboots as he was known, who took control. They completed the 1956 series victory, 3-1, at Eden Park (see G for Grounds) with an 11-5 win. South Africa were defeated in a Test series for the first time – by any side – in 60 years. The All Blacks followed this up in 1959 with a 3-1 series victory over the Lions.

Feared the world over the 1967 team inspired the greatest run of consecutive wins in the history of All Black rugby. They went 17 Tests, from 1965 to

NEW ZEALAND

▲ Graham
Mourie, captain of
the 1978 All Black
Grand Slam side.

1969 without losing a single one. Brian Lochore's 1967 All Blacks are thought to be the finest New Zealand side of all time and when they arrived in the British Isles, just one draw, against East Wales, prevented a perfect record.

Lochore was appointed New Zealand captain – for the 4-0 victory over the Lions in 1966 – following the retirement of Wilson Whineray. In those days the announcement of the new All Blacks captain ranked up there with the announcement of a new Prime Minister.

In the 1970s the All Blacks had two almighty series with the Lions but when the 1978 team arrived in Europe records tumbled. Graham Mourie's 1978 All Blacks became the first to complete a Grand Slam in Britain and Ireland. They beat Wales 13-12, Ireland 10-6, England 16-6 and Scotland 18-9. The only side to beat them on their 18-match tour were Munster.

Outside of the Test scene members of the New Zealand Rugby Union regarded the domestic challenge competition, the Ranfurly Shield as important. But in the modern era they realised that it wasn't enough to provide competition for their domestic sides. So in 1976 they decided to form the National Provincial Championship, allowing all 27 unions to compete in three divisions.

Without formal leagues in Britain until the 1980s the establishment of the NPC was ground-breaking. This fiercely-fought competition helped New Zealand reach the top of the world game in the 1980s.

Considering New Zealand's position through rugby's history it was fitting that they lifted the first Rugby World Cup, in 1987 (see W for World Cup).

The 1987 side took the loss of its captain Andy Dalton in its stride before the tournament, immediately finding another great leader in David Kirk to take them into battle. From John Gallagher at full-back to John Kirwan on the wing Kirk's side dominated the tournament. From the first game when they beat Italy 70-6, to the last where they overcame the impressive France side, 29-9, it was New Zealand all the way. The 20-point margin in the final was the closest any side got to beating the 1987 All Blacks.

THE A TO Z OF RUGBY

New Zealand failed to repeat the win in 1991 and at the 2003 World Cup had to settle for their second successive exit at the semi-final stage.

At the 2003 World Cup they won back some pride with a third/fourth place play-off win over France but their semi-final exit to Australia still cost coach John Mitchell his job. Mitchell was soon replaced by former Lions and Wales coach Graham Henry, who didn't take long moving New Zealand back to No 1 in the world.

Henry masterminded a stellar season in 2005, hammering the Lions 3-0 in a record-breaking Test series, taking the Tri Nations and then completing a Grand Slam tour of the home nations.

In 2006, they again took the Tri Nations Series by winning their first five matches, (three against Australia and two against South Africa). However, they lost their final match of the series against South Africa. They completed their end of year tour unbeaten, with record away wins over France, England and Wales. The All Blacks were named 2006 IRB Team of the Year and were nominated for the Laureus World Sports Award for the second time, while flanker Richie McCaw was named IRB Player of the Year.

The All Blacks entered the 2007 Rugby World Cup as favourites, and trumped their pool beating all their challengers, Scotland, Italy, Romania and Portugal by 40 points or more. However, they then suffered a defeat to hosts France in the first knockout game, the quarter-finals.

Nonetheless the All Blacks have a positive win record against every nation they have played and, with the exception of South Africa, have a winning margin of over 65% for every other country. They have won 323 of the 434 matches played, a win percentage of 74.6%. By this measure, the All Blacks are the most successful international rugby union team in history.

▲ Happy faces from the All Blacks after beating the Wallabies in the Bledisloe Cup, 2008.

Oxford and Cambridge

► The 1922 Cambridge team at Crystal Palace for the inter Varsity Match.

The second Tuesday in December when Oxford take on Cambridge in the Varsity Match at Twickenham is one of English rugby's great social occasions. The car parks at HQ are full of the hampers and champers brigade, determined to have a good day out as always, but on the pitch things have changed slightly over the years. With the onset of professionalism and the academies set up by the clubs around the country, you are less likely to spot a future international playing in this historic game than you were in the past. Fortunately, that does not deter thousands of spectators from turning up and having a huge pre-Christmas party.

It may be an anachronism in these days of eye coaches and nutritionists, but it is a good excuse for current students, past scholars and interested neutrals to let their hair down and have a few beers. The roll of honour is impressive with players such as Rob Andrew, Stuart Barnes, Gerald Davies, Chris Oti, Rob Wainwright and Gavin Hastings all playing in the game, as did BBC radio rugby commentator Ian Robertson in 1967. Robertson's colleague Alastair Hignell, who also went on to play for his country, scored a record 45 points in four Varsity Matches between 1974 and 1977. Three other

▲ Charlie
Desmond of
Cambridge scores
the equalising try
during the 2003
Varsity Match .

famous names – Phil Horrocks-Taylor (1956), Gareth Rees (1994) and David Humphreys (1995) – each scored "full houses" of a try, drop goal, conversion and penalty in Varsity games.

The first Varsity Match was played in February 1872 at "the Parks" in Oxford after Cambridge initiated the fixture and it has been played every year ever since, barring the periods covered by the two World Wars. Oxford won the first match and Cambridge the second with the next two drawn, and the two sides were neck and neck until the 1990s

when the light blues of Cambridge won a succession of matches. Of the 122 games played up to December 2003, Oxford had won 51 and Cambridge 57. There had been 14 draws, including the 2003 match that ended 11-11, but Cambridge did not take the lead in the series until 1981.

In 1873 the match was played in Cambridge before it was decided to move it to the Kennington Oval and up until 1875, when the fixture was made 15-a-side, the teams fielded 20 players each. Several games were played at Queen's Club in Fulham before, in 1921, the match was moved to Twickenham.

In the early 1970s, the fixture was in the doldrums until an insurance company, Bowring, took over the sponsorship. The universities started to recruit more mature students with rugby pedigrees and the fixture recovered. It is now played in front of a near full-house every year for the MMC (Marsh and McLennan) Trophy. The firm had merged with Bowring in 1980.

Every player in the Varsity Match receives his Blue (dark blue for Oxford and light blue for Cambridge), but rugby struggled initially to get full Blue status. The Cambridge Rugby Club applied for the full status in 1883, but Reginald Gridley, the university boat club president, and the athletics and cricket clubs put up a host of objections to rugby being granted the same status as cricket and rowing. The president was apparently not impressed that thousands of people went to watch the Varsity rugby match and that the sides fielded international players. He decided that the rugby union and football clubs should share a number of full Blues between them.

The rugby and soccer sides disagreed with this and the next year they awarded themselves Blues, forcing the Boat Club to bring the dispute before the whole university in an open debate at the Union. A huge audience saw the Boat Club back down and finally agree to award Blues for rugby union and football.

There have been many bizarre and memorable games between the two great universities over the years. For instance in 1920 Oxford were captained by the South African Denoon Duncan who took the unusual step of selecting Boet Neser, a prop, at fly-half. The modern philosophy of a player not taking any notice of the number on his back and playing total rugby had been bought into even in those days! But confounding all expectations, Neser made the first try and scored the last. Unsurprisingly, the game is known as "Neser's match".

There have been murmurs that the universities are recruiting too many foreign players just to play in the match, but that is nothing new. In 1953, the Oxford side had nine overseas players, including seven from South Africa. That year's Dark Blue vintage were dubbed "Springboxford".

Aside from their day in the sun, or more usually driving rain, in December, the universities have contributed hugely to English rugby. William Webb Ellis, who supposedly "picked up the ball and ran" in the first place, was a student at Brasenose College and the Oxford University Rugby Football Club was founded in 1869, about 15 months before the RFU, and is regarded as the oldest club in England.

Cambridge University Rugby Union Club was officially formed in 1872 and club officials helped to draw up the laws of rugby, which were adopted by the RFU. It became a Constituent Body of the Union

▼ A minute's silence is held in memory of Ian Tucker prior to the 1996 Varsity Match.

in 1872 and in 1896 started playing matches at the famous Grange Road.

Oxford's ground at Iffley Road is graced by the Ian Tucker Memorial Statue, a tribute to the player who died after being injured playing for the Dark Blues against Saracens in 1996. The names of the Best and Fairest player from the Blues XV each year are inscribed on the monument and the Ian Tucker Foundation raises awareness of sports-related brain injuries.

In 2005 South African Rudi Bosch scored two tries as Cambridge beat Oxford 31-16, in front of 38,733 fans… and he became the first man to be shown the yellow card in the Varsity Match.

In 2006, Cambridge University won 44-0. This was the first ever nilling in the history of the match, and it was the biggest margin of victory as well but Oxford gained some small measure of revenge with back-to-back victories in the following years.

▶ Success for Cambridge at the 2007 Varsity Match.

Pienaar

▲ The most famous picture in rugby as Francois Pienaar accepts the 1995 Rugby World Cup trophy from Nelson Mandela.

In every generation there are sportsmen who transcend the game changing it, on and off the pitch, forever. One such man was Jacobus "Francois" Pienaar.

Pienaar, born in January 1967, was the man charged with the responsibility of taking South African rugby, not only out of isolation, but into a new era when they would host the third Rugby World Cup.

South African sport had been left in the wilderness for almost a decade. Banned from international competition because of worldwide opposition to their political system, Apartheid, which promoted a divided society, the Springboks were unable to play any official rugby Test matches.

So when they were re-admitted the game in the Republic needed not just a mere player, but a statesman and a role model for a new generation into the bargain. They got it with Pienaar.

One of the game's most enduring images is of Pienaar at the end of the 1995 Rugby World Cup, with the Webb Ellis Cup, alongside the country's new President Nelson Mandela, who was dressed in Pienaar's famous No 6 shirt. Pienaar was quite simply one of the most important figures in the history of rugby union.

▼ Hennie Muller leads his legendary Springbok side out to face Scotland in 1951. The Scots were thrashed 44-0 .

South Africa's role in rugby union had been central since their first Test match in 1891 and so powerful were they as a rugby playing nation that it took England until 1969 to actually beat them.

So when the sporting boycott, because of the Apartheid regime, began to bite, it hit rugby union perhaps the hardest of all sports, as it removed one of the most powerful countries from the game.

That rugby boycott was in place in the late-1980s, ensuring that South Africa, who would have been one of the favourites, missed the first two World Cups in 1987 and 1991.

But after Apartheid was smashed and Nelson Mandela made his unforgettable Walk to Freedom, in 1990, it was time to begin their re-integration back into the world of sport. The ban was lifted in 1992, and they returned to international rugby.

The International Rugby Board set the ball rolling by offering the new South Africa, the Rainbow Nation, the 1995 World Cup. It was then that Pienaar began to leave his indelible mark on the sport.

As the South African Springboks had been unable to play serious international rugby for almost a decade, Pienaar came into that World Cup as captain, with only 16 caps to his name. He galvanised not only a team but also a nation behind the men in green.

"Amongst sporting leaders, Francois Pienaar stands out. It was under his inspiring leadership that rugby, a sport previously associated with one sector of our population and with a particular brand of politics, became the pride of their entire country," the country's president, Mandela wrote in the book *Rainbow Warrior*.

"A beacon in our process of nation-building will always remain the

Springboks under his captaincy winning the World Cup in 1995. Seldom before or since has the country celebrated in such harmony and togetherness. Francois Pienaar's leadership extended way beyond the rugby field, and he truly represented all South Africans."

The thing that makes Pienaar stand head and shoulders above other rugby captains and coaches is the effect he had on the wider political world. He did so much to ease South Africa back into international sport after years on the sidelines due to Apartheid.

Due to this isolation Pienaar had a relatively short international career, playing just 29 times for his country, although it says much for his abilities that he captained the Springboks in each of those 29 Tests, losing just eight.

A distinguished sporting career in his teens led Pienaar to be at the forefront of a powerful Transvaal side in the early 1990s, when he earned his reputation.

▲ South African fans enjoy the opening ceremony of the 1995 Rugby World Cup.

▲ Francois
Pienaar in Pretoria,
1994.

In 1993 a Transvaal side with Pienaar as the captain won the inaugural Super 10 competition (a forerunner to the Super 12). They also picked up consecutive Currie Cup titles in 1993 and 1994.

During this time Pienaar forged a formidable partnership with Kitch Christie, the man who was to coach the Springboks at the 1995 World Cup. So Pienaar became the one and only choice as captain for that tournament.

The appointment of Andre Markgraaf as Springbok coach after the 1995 World Cup led to Pienaar's departure from South Africa and a famous sojourn in England.

Markgraaf had told Pienaar he would not figure in his plans and as the coach had been appointed, at the time, until the end of the 1999 World Cup it was clear that Pienaar needed to search for pastures new.

"I took the news on the chin, but I was hurt, I felt so bad, so miserable," he admitted. "Adding insult to injury the coach had not even telephoned me with the news."

Predictably that announcement was greeted with astonishment across South Africa. Radio phone-ins and TV debates were packed with people who could not believe Pienaar had been axed.

Many believed Pienaar had been dropped as he was "too strong" for coach Markgraaf but whatever the reasons it was clear his days in South

Africa were numbered.

Markgraaf's decision was hardly borne out by results and a year later the Springboks went down to the British and Irish Lions, without Pienaar.

Pienaar was still keen to win his place back but the crucial intervention came from his World Cup coach, Kitch Christie. He told Pienaar to seriously consider the offer from English club Saracens, suggesting he would relish a new challenge.

In taking on that new challenge, Pienaar was lucky in that leaving South Africa he was able to join Nigel Wray's Saracens, a club steeped in history and owned by a man who loved the spirit of rugby.

A multi-millionaire, Wray is full of humility and even waited at Heathrow Airport for two hours to collect Pienaar and his wife, Nerine, on their arrival in England.

Pienaar finished off his playing career with Saracens, later becoming Chief Executive of Watford-based Premiership club, delivering the Tetley's Bitter Cup for them in 1998 before leaving in 2002, his footprints indelibly left in rugby's history.

▲ Holding the Tetley's Bitter Cup trophy.

◀ Francois Pienaar on the ball against Wasps in the 1998 Tetley's Bitter Cup.

Quinnell

▶ Father of the dynasty – Derek Quinnell – on the ball with the 1974 Lions.

▼ Derek Quinnell waits for a Welsh ball in 1980.

The name Quinnell has been toasted and revered throughout the game, most notably in the clubhouses and alehouses of West Wales, for nigh on 35 years as one of the most famous dynasties in the rugby world.

The sweat and commitment of a life of toil at rugby's coalface has been shared across these decades by father Derek and sons Scott and Craig. And there is little likelihood that the pedigree of this most aristocratic of rugby bloodlines will diminish over the next few years with youngest scion Gavin already capped at under-21 level.

Throw in the fact that the wondrous fly-half Barry "King" John, whose peerless talents flickered all too briefly on the international stage, is Derek's brother-in-law and the three

lads' uncle and the Principality can claim with some justification to have an alternative Royal Family.

To pick up the story from its early days, a raw-boned, red-haired back-row forward from Stradey Park, barely 22, was a surprise selection for the British and Irish Lions tour of New Zealand in 1971.

Carwyn James, the party's inspirational coach, saw something in the young man from Llanelli which had eluded the Welsh selectors up to that point. And the heroic greenhorn played a pivotal role, persistently collaring the dangerous All Blacks' scrum-half Sid Going in what turned out to be a triumphant and historic tour.

A Lion he may have been, but Derek remained uncapped by Wales until the dying moments of the following year's Five Nations' championship. Finally, the great No 8 Mervyn Davies had to leave the field due to injury late in the game against France at Cardiff. Desperate to get on to the (Arms) park, young Derek muscled his way past battalions of Welsh constabulary, as well as the touch judge, to reach his promised land just before the referee blew for time.

Derek went on to win 23 caps with Wales and take part in two further Lions tours – to South Africa in 1974 and New Zealand three years later. However, he is likely to be best remembered for his mighty contribution to two matches which have never been accorded international status but will live forever in rugby's collective consciousness.

Llanelli's 9-3 victory over the 1972-73 All Blacks owed much to Derek's commitment to the cause and knowledge of his opponents. Arguably, this is still the Scarlets' finest hour in front of their saucepan-worshipping fans.

A few weeks later, against the same opponents, he produced an equally telling performance for the Barbarians in a 23-11 victory regarded by many pundits as perhaps the greatest match ever played.

After his Llanelli team-mate Phil Bennett had sold not one but two dummies in front of his own posts early in proceedings, a staggering passage of play unfolded. At a crucial moment, Quinnell brilliantly took a pass at ankle height and off-loaded with aplomb. Seconds later, with Cliff Morgan drooling so lyrically in his BBC commentary, Gareth Edwards sprinted 10 yards to set the seal on a truly immortal try-scoring move.

Fast forward to the early 1990s, and the name Quinnell once again featured in the back-rows of both Llanelli and Wales.

▼ Scott Quinnell heads to the line to score his famous touchline try against France in 1994.

Q

► Gavin Quinnell playing for Llanelli against Newport, October 2003.

▼ Scott and Craig celebrate Wales' famous Wembley victory against England in 1999.

Eldest son Scott, now retired, made his international debut at No 8 against Canada late in 1993 and went on to score the try of the 1994 Five Nations' tournament as Wales clinched the title with a 24–15 victory over France in Cardiff.

The young buffalo at the base of the Welsh scrum was absolutely rampant that day and immediately found himself being compared with his father.

The arguments still rage as to whether Derek or Scott was the better

player, but there is no doubt that at his peak Scott was a world–class No 8 whose bulldozing style gained the hard yards that were so valuable for every team in which he played. In retrospect, it is no surprise that these talents soon attracted offers from rugby league.

After his triumphant 1993-94 season, Scott, with a wife and baby to support, had little choice but to turn his

back on a game that was still amateur and opt for the financial security of a £500,000 transfer to Wigan.

Scott's absence from rugby union lasted two years, but once professionalism had dawned in the wake of the 1995 World Cup he was back plying his trade with Richmond, a traditional London club awash with new money which eventually led it to ruin.

He won his 10th cap for Wales against the United States in January 1997 and went to South Africa with the Lions the following summer only for a groin injury to end his tour before the start of the Test series.

The injury niggled for another year before eventually clearing up. But it was a move back to Llanelli during the early part of the 1998-99 season which provided the impetus Scott's career had lacked at Richmond.

He was back to his best during the 1999 Five Nations and World Cup campaigns. He had the unenviable distinction of being the first player to be sin-binned in a Test against France but a year later captained Wales to their only victory over the Springboks.

Another Lions tour, to Australia, beckoned in 2001 and this time Scott played all three Tests – a series that the visitors were a trifle unlucky to lose 2-1. Then, at the end of the following season, he announced his retirement from the Welsh team after 52 caps and 11 tries, citing the increasing physical difficulty he encountered in giving his all for both club and country.

Scott continued to play for Llanelli

– and was part of the Scarlets team that won the Celtic League title in 2004 – before announcing his retirement from rugby union at the end of the 2004-05 season.

Brother Craig, now in his mid-30s, looked likely to have a similar impact to Scott when he made his debut against Fiji in 1995, aged only 20. But it took another three years, by which time he too had moved from Llanelli to Richmond, before he became established in Wales' second-row.

When Richmond merged with London Irish and London Scottish in May 1999, Craig moved back to Wales, but instead of rejoining Llanelli, as Scott had, he went to Cardiff. He won the last of his 32 caps in 2002 with some observers close to the game feeling that his sheer size (he is 6' 6" and weighs more than 20 stone) counted against him in a game which is dominated nowadays by fitness and mobility.

On 13 April 2006 Craig announced his retirement from professional rugby following a neck injury sustained during a game for Cardiff against Glasgow Warriors. Doctors told him that he risked being in a wheelchair if he played rugby again.

◀ Craig Quinnell in action for Cardiff before his retirement.

Record Breakers

Will Carling runs through the heart of the Welsh defence during England's 1995 Grand Slam campaign.

1. MOST TESTS AS A CAPTAIN
Will Carling (England) – 59

Will Carling led England through the most successful period in their history, winning Grand Slams in 1991, 1992 and 1995 and taking them to a World Cup final in 1991.

Born in Bradford-on-Avon, Carling was handed the captaincy in the same year, 1988, as he made his England debut, aged just 22.

Undoubtedly Carling was lucky to preside over an exceptionally gifted group of players but he still captained the side a record 59 times and his role in England's heyday should not be underestimated. Current Newcastle coach Rob Andrew was Carling's outside-half in the glory days.

"Will bore the responsibility of being captain superbly," said Andrew. "As a centre he had great pace and power, qualities which were the perfect foil to Jeremy Guscott.

"It's difficult to find a weakness in his game."

The career of the Harlequins centre was not without controversy as he was sacked from the England captaincy when he called the RFU committee "57 old farts" in an off the cuff remark at the end of an interview in May 1995.

But after uproar and the refusal of any other England player to take on the captaincy Carling was reinstated in an embarrassing U-turn for the RFU.

He failed to make the step-up to a Lions career, dropping out with injury after being selected for the 1989 tour and failing to win a Test match spot four years later.

Carling made the last of 72 Test appearances in 1997.

2. MOST TEST MATCH TRIES
David Campese (Australia) – 64

Before, during and after David Campese's 15-year international career he managed to pick up a few enemies along the way with his outspoken views. It must irk those enemies and fans of every nation, apart from Australia, that the wing from Randwick had the ability to walk the walk as well as talk the talk.

An on-field entertainer Campese certainly knew the way to the try line, crossing it 64 times in his 101 Tests, a remarkable strike rate in such a long career.

Campo, as he was universally known, perfected the goose-step. Not to be confused with the side-step, Campese's trick was his change of pace and for more than a decade it left international opponents trailing in the dirt.

A World Cup winner in 1991 many people believe that it was the way Campese taunted England that made them change from their tried and tested forward game plan to one of an expansive nature in the final.

He was voted the Player of the Tournament at the 1991 World Cup and if he didn't score in the final he certainly left his mark on the semi-final win over New Zealand.

Always with one eye on the unconsidered option, Campese didn't always get it right as Greg Martin will testify. The Wallaby wing threw Martin a risky pass near his own try line against

▲ David Campese leaves the field after his final match for Australia against the Barbarians in 1996.

◀ A young David Campese (centre) running in a try for the Australian touring team of 1984.

▲ George Gregan spins the ball out during the 1999 Rugby World Cup semi-final against South Africa.

the 1989 Lions. The ball went loose, Ieuan Evans pounced and the series went to the British and Irish visitors.

Campese made his debut against New Zealand in 1982, immediately opening his account with a sensational try and by the time he arrived in Europe with the 1984 Grand Slam side his place as a rugby legend was guaranteed.

After he retired Campese managed the Australian Sevens squad to a bronze medal at the 1998 Commonwealth Games and in January 2002 was awarded his Order of Australia Medal (AM) for services to Rugby Union.

3. MOST CAPPED SCRUM-HALF
George Gregan (Australia) – 139

When Nick Farr-Jones retired from the Australia No 9 shirt it was always going to take a big player to fill those big shoes.

But in ACT Brumbies scrum-half George Gregan, Australia found not only a superb replacement but a man who went on to win more Test caps than any No 9 before him.

Gregan was the lynchpin of one of the most successful international teams of the 1990s, winning the World Cup (1999) and Tri Nations titles before being instrumental in Australia's series against the Lions, in 2001.

Only the presence of the unforgettable John Eales as Australian captain prevented Gregan from getting his hands on the Wallaby armband until Eales' retirement in 2001, although he was vice captain for the four years before.

Born in Zambia, Gregan made his debut in 1994 against Italy and became one of the most accomplished players of his generation, becoming the world's most-capped player, in any position, overtaking Jason Leonard's record of 114 caps, in 2005.

He initially made his name on the Sevens circuit and was also an accomplished cricketer.

Gregan was responsible for one of the most famous tackles in the history of the game, knocking the ball out of the hands of All Blacks wing Jeff Wilson as he was about to score a try to win the Bledisloe Cup in 1994.

Like Gareth Edwards in the 1970s Gregan was a devastating attacking threat, as well as being a great passer of the ball. In defence he has the ability to stop anyone.

4. MOST CONSECUTIVE TESTS
Sean Fitzpatrick (New Zealand) – 63

One of the greatest players to pull on an All Blacks jersey, once Sean Fitzpatrick made his Test debut in 1986 there was hardly any shifting him from the team.

The son of All Black centre Brian, Sean got his chance in the Test arena after the rebel Cavaliers tour to South Africa. Following that game the New Zealand Rugby Union picked a side, in 1986, dubbed The Baby Blacks of which Sean was a key component.

Fitzy's career saw him win 92 caps, while his run of 63 consecutive games saw him stay in the New Zealand team for a remarkable eight years. He enjoyed series wins against all the major nations and a World Cup final win in 1987. Fitzy also captained his country a record 51 times.

The run that allows him to take his place in our list of record breakers would have gone on but the Auckland hooker was rested for an easy game, against Japan, in the 1995 World Cup pool stage.

As strong a scrummager as most props, Fitzy was a massive presence around the field and in the line-out for the All Blacks. He was the world's most-capped forward until Jason Leonard took his record. But by the end of the 2003 World Cup no other hooker had played more Tests.

A knee injury eventually ended his international career in 1997 and the All Blacks have struggled to replace him ever since.

In the *New Zealand Rugby Greats* book former New Zealand coach Laurie Mains said of him;

"Following the tour of Australia and South Africa in 1992 it was obvious he was something special. He possessed the almost indefinable X-factor of which great All Black captains are made."

▼ Sean Fitzpatrick on line-out duty.

Six Nations

The most famous and oldest rugby tournament in the world, the Six Nations championship is revered throughout the rugby world.

The championship, now contested by England, France, Ireland, Scotland, Wales and Italy, embodies everything great about the game of rugby union and ensures hundreds of thousands of people pack into European stadiums every Spring.

Rugby's first international, between England and Scotland was staged in 1871. Although those two sides plus Ireland and Wales played each other regularly, the championship didn't get it's moniker of the Five Nations until 1910, when the French were invited into the annual rugby festival.

France's first game was a trip to Swansea to take on Wales, a difficult start considering Wales' domination in the decade before. But the French managed, at least, to get on the scoreboard, although they did lose 49-14.

The French haven't conceded so many points in a championship game since and their 37-0 defeat against England a year later, in 1911, remains their biggest loss.

The years before the war essentially belonged to England as they only lost three games in the three years before 1914, taking three titles between 1910 and 1914.

After staging rugby's first international in 1871, Scotland spent much of the intervening period as the bridesmaids of European rugby. In the 1920s that changed as they lifted their first Grand Slam.

More than 70,000 people crowded into Murrayfield in 1925 to see Scotland win 14-11.

France were in their 18th championship before they claimed their first victory over England, in 1927, and it came by the slim margin of 3-0.

That French success was followed by a period of isolation. Amid allegations of professionalism in the French Leagues the national side was excluded from the championship in the 1930s and they didn't return to the tournament until after the Second World War, in 1946.

In the last championship before the War, Wales, Ireland and England shared the title; all three sides lost one match.

Despite having some great teams in the last century, the Irish side have only managed to deliver one Grand Slam, in 1948. Some 32,000 people packed into Ravenhill to see Ireland clinch their first Grand Slam with a 6-3 victory over Wales. Outside-half Jackie Kyle and hooker Karl Mullen were at the centre of so much of the brilliant Irish play and the side scored 10 tries in their four games, more than they'd achieved for 20 years.

The Welsh were also moving into a dominant period in their history, winning Grand Slams in 1950 and 1952 while only being out of the first two in the championship once in the 1950s. England also enjoyed success later in the decade, taking their own Grand Slam in 1957.

In the 1960s Wales and France dominated the championship, with seven outright wins between them.

France's greatest day arrived in 1968. A year after winning the championship again they finally completed their first Grand Slam.

When you mention the 1970s one vision comes into the minds of rugby fans everywhere – Wales. From 1969 to 1979, Wales came to power in the Five Nations and this time will be

◀ England celebrate at the final whistle, after winning the 2003 Grand Slam.

▼ Scotland vs Wales from 1927, the year Scotland and Ireland tied the Five Nations.

remembered as the golden era of Welsh rugby.

Winning the Triple Crown six times, the Welsh side were almost unstoppable. Only an outstanding French side prevented them from adding to the three Grand Slams achieved in this decade, with their own in 1977.

In 1976 Wales were at their best. Their lowest score in 1976 was 19 points and no side scored more than 13 points against them. Their total of 102 points was a championship record.

One of the most endearing pictures in rugby's history shows one William (or Bill to everyone in the rugby world) Beaumont being chaired off the pitch, at Murrayfield, after England had clinched their first Grand Slam for 23 years, in 1980.

The four victories were built on the incredible England pack that not only delivered the Grand Slam but a prized and rare victory in the Parc des Princes (17-13), their first in Paris for 16 years. The success was, however, isolated for England and it was France who took over the decade, winning the

▲ Welsh captain John Dawes chaired off the pitch after Wales' 1971 Grand Slam winning victory in France.

title outright three times. The French feat included two Grand Slams and they even shared the title three more times.

It was left to Scotland to put down the real challenge to the French and in 1984 came their first Grand Slam for 46 years.

The final game in 1984 was the Grand Slam decider with both Scotland and France still unbeaten. Scotland triumphed 21-12 after falling 9-3 behind but being allowed back into the match by French indiscipline.

Ireland won the Triple Crown and the championship, in 1985, with a 13-10 Dublin win over England, and it was Tom Kiernan who proved the hero dropping a vital, injury time, goal.

As Wales did in the 1970s so England started the 1990s winning the Grand Slam three times. They marked their dominance by taking the Triple Crown six times in eight seasons. They did it under one captain, Will Carling.

The 1991 Grand Slam was achieved after they won a two-way battle with the French, the crucial victory coming at Twickenham, 21-19. In 1992 they flew through the other four nations, scoring a championship record 118 points (35 more than in 1991), only conceding 29 on their way to the Slam, scoring 15 tries.

The following year – 1993 – brought only two wins for Carling and they had to wait until 1995 for their final Grand Slam of the decade, and until Martin Johnson's side won it the next time, in 2003.

England may have dominated the middle period of the decade but they didn't get the start they needed. Scotland won the Grand Slam in 1990, again with a winner takes all showdown, with England on the final day of the championship.

Scotland also ended the decade on top, clinching the 1999 Five Nations with a last weekend victory over the French, in Paris.

Wales had limped through the 1980s but worse was to come in 1990 when they suffered their first whitewash in the Five Nations.

Under the captaincy of Ieuan Evans they did buck the trend once, in 1994, when they were Five Nations champions, losing one game, but winning it on a superior points difference.

Wales may have had little to cheer for in the 1990s but they ended the

decade on a high. With Cardiff Arms Park being redeveloped, Wales had decamped to Wembley for their home games. It was Clive Woodward's England, captained by Lawrence Dallaglio who arrived, hunting a Grand Slam.

With a Scott Gibbs try in the dying seconds, Wales delivered a sensational 32-31 victory.

Points difference was introduced to separate the teams in 1993, although it wasn't needed to decide the winner in that year, France taking the title with three wins.

France had to wait until the end of the decade to assert their supremacy on the Five Nations, taking back-to-back Grand Slams in 1997 and 1998.

In 1997 the records tumbled as the sides scored 53 tries and an incredible

▲ Another iconic rugby photograph sees Bill Beaumont chaired off the Murrayfield pitch after England's victory secured the 1980 Grand Slam.

▼ France beating
Scotland to win
the Six Nations in
2007.

511 points in 10 matches. This smashed the previous best of 363, six years before.

France repeated the Grand Slam in 1998, in a championship which saw Sunday play for the first time and a year later Lloyds-TSB paid £12 million for the privilege of sponsoring the title for the next two seasons.

Five became six in 2000, when Italy offered the Five Nations committee a proven club championship, good competition for their national sides and a venue, in Rome, that their supporters were dying to get to.

Although it took Italy until 2000 to kick off the Six Nations they did it in dramatic style, beating Scotland 34-20.

They couldn't follow-up that win and the Italians lost 14 consecutive games. However, their fortunes took an upward turn in 2003 with their best championship performance, beating Wales and scoring a very respectable 100 points in their five games.

Clive Woodward's England ended four years of near misses by finally winning a Grand Slam in 2003. Between 1999 and 2002 England had a shocking record in the last game of the championship. In three of those four years they won all their games before falling at the final hurdle.

In 1999 it was Wales, 2000 Scotland and 2001 Ireland who beat them in the final match, although in 2002 France showed their abilities with a Grand Slam. Those bad memories for the English team were banished to the history books in 2003. In this year Ireland and England arrived at the last game – again in Dublin – both unbeaten in a winner takes all Grand Slam showdown.

It was the first time, since 1995, that the Grand Slam (when England beat Scotland) could have been won by either team playing in the last match. Once again England held their nerve, this time to triumph 42-6, Will Greenwood scoring two tries.

After England's World Cup win in 2003 their Six Nations form plummeted seeing them finish outside the top two in 2004, 2005 and 2006.

Wales pulled off their first Grand Slam since 1978 with a sensational clean sweep in 2005 and a year later it was France's turn to lift the trophy, after losing their opening game to Scotland. Ireland picked up second and a Triple Crown with a last-minute, 28-24 victory over England, Shane Horgan grabbing the winning try in the eighth minute of injury time.

In 2007, France again won on points difference, after four teams had at least a mathematical chance of topping the table going into the final week. The Italians had their first away win of the tournament beating Scotland in Edinburgh. It was also the first time they won two of their matches as they went on to beat Wales in Rome.

▲ Wales outclass France on their way to winning the 2008 Grand Slam.

Scotland won the wooden spoon and Ireland won the Triple Crown for the second straight year and third time in four years.

In 2008, Wales – under new head coach Warren Gatland and part-time defence coach Shaun Edwards – won the Grand Slam with a 29-12 win against France in Cardiff, having only conceded two tries in the championship, beating England's previous record of four tries conceded.

Tri Nations

With the dawn of professional rugby in 1995 it was inevitable that the game would engineer more high class and regular competition between nations and leading clubs.

The Northern Hemisphere had established their Five Nations in 1910 and although those in the south had survived on a diet of tours and the World Cup, it was only a matter of time before an annual competition was established.

There were fears that this regular competition would become stale but the Tri Nations tournament, between Australia, South Africa and New Zealand, has been a huge success, each July and August.

Inevitably the new tournament – which kicked off in 1996 – has produced some great matches and when *Rugby World* magazine declared its best

match of the period between 1990 and 2002, it was New Zealand's win over Australia at the opening of Stadium Australia, in 2000. In a ding-dong battle the All Blacks eventually snatched it 39-35.

With such long distances to travel – unlike in the Six Nations – the draw is all-important. New Zealand and Australia play their games in South Africa back-to-back and if the Springboks can get those games at the short of the hat-trick. The new, exciting South African team won every game in 1998 (their only Grand Slam), including a 29-15 victory in the last match against Australia.

In 1999 with the Rugby World Cup just around the corner normal Tri Nations service was resumed with New Zealand topping the table. They made it despite a last weekend defeat to Australia, 28-7, in front of an astonishing 107,052 fans at Stadium Australia. The Wallabies would have taken the title with that win were it not for their thrilling 10-9 defeat in South Africa.

With the World Cup safely tucked up in the offices of the Australian Rugby Union it was probably fitting that they followed up this success by winning their first Tri Nations trophy, in 2000.

To win the World Cup is the ultimate sign of success. To follow it up 10 months later with the Tri Nations ensured that this Australian team would be ranked among the best the world has ever seen. Captain John

◀ Jonah Lomu evades the tackle of Stephen Larkham during their Bledisloe Cup match at Stadium Australia, 2000. New Zealand won the epic match 39-35.

▼ Christian Cullen of New Zealand is tackled by Andre Venter of South Africa during their 1997 Tri Nations match.

start of the tournament it increases their chances of getting off to a flying start.

From the outset the Tri Nations broke new ground with bonus points for tries scored. Although you didn't need recourse to a calculator to see who'd won it in the first year (1996) as New Zealand were victorious in all four of their matches. Australia in particular were beaten 43-6 in that year.

The All Blacks made it two titles out of two, in 1997, but they fell a long way

▲ Toutai Kefu bulldozes over the line for the try that secured the 2001 Tri Nations title.

For the second successive year Australia overcame defeat in their first game, this time 20-15 to South Africa, to win the Tri Nations.

As if to stress how hard it is to take the upper hand in the Southern Hemisphere a monumental New Zealand effort in 2002 prevented the Australians from completing the hat-trick. Again the champions failed to win every game, the All Blacks suffering a 16-14 reversal in Australia. New Zealand did beat them 12-6 when the sides met for the first game of the tournament.

The Springboks struggled in the initial years of the Tri Nations and in 2002 they finished bottom again, this time with one win, 33-31 against Australia.

The last Tri Nations tournament before the 2003 World Cup ended with a victory for New Zealand over Australia, a triumph that All Blacks failed to repeat in the World Cup semi-finals.

In 2004 South Africa claimed their first Tri Nations title since 1998 with a superb second half performance to beat Australia 23-19 and leave the All Blacks bottom, but in 2005 New Zealand

Eales said; "The great thing is there's so much depth in Australian rugby, a lot more than we had a few years ago. The Tri Nations showed that the new generation is just around the corner and coming through fast."

In 2001 Australia completed an incredible double, beating the British and Irish Lions 2-1 in their Test series and then going on to retain the Tri Nations in an incredible few months of rugby for the Wallabies.

This time, in 2001, they needed a late, late try from Toutai Kefu to get a 29-26 win over New Zealand and they lifted the trophy, before their captain John Eales, retired.

began their rise to the world's best side, by winning the trophy four years in a row. The All Blacks' narrow victory over Australia in September 2008 also secured the trans-Tasman Bledisloe Cup for the sixth straight year.

The competition was expanded in 2006 with each of the three nations playing each other three times, although the 2007 series reverted to a double round-robin to reduce fixture congestion in a World Cup year.

Historically there have been persistent rumours about the inclusion of Argentina into this competition but no official word has ever been released.

If the Tri Nations satisfied the need for great international competition the Super 12 bridged the gap between domestic competition and Test matches.

When professionalism arrived in rugby union in 1995 the Southern Hemisphere was far quicker out of the starting blocks than their counterparts in the north. Crucial to this strategy was a top class tournament that fed the national teams. The progress of the current Super 12 started in the mid-1980s with the South Pacific Championships or Super 6. This early tournament even involved Fiji but the

▲ The Australian team poses one day ahead of its Tri Nations match against South Africa, June 2007.

Super 12 is now restricted to the best provinces from Australia, New Zealand and South Africa.

After a break forced on the organisers by the withdrawal of New South Wales, the competition was relaunched as a Super 10, in 1993, comprising of four sides from New Zealand, three from South Africa, two from Australia and one from the Pacific Islands, which this time was Western Samoa.

That 1993 final – after the sides were split into two pools – was won by Transvaal (South Africa) who beat Auckland 20-17.

The official declaration of professional rugby allowed the tournament to take its current shape and it was renamed Super 12.

The omission of a Pacific Island team – and the increase to 12 sides – allowed the big three an additional side each in

► Action from the 2008 Tri Nations match between the Springboks and the Wallabies.

the new revamped tournament.

The clamour for an Islands team to be reinstated into a new Super 14 was deafening at the 2003 Rugby World Cup. Auckland were the first Super 12 winners, with the tournament in a one pool league, beating Natal 45-21 in the final.

From its inception it has become a pioneering tournament. They were the first to offer a bonus for tries scored and started a scoring system that was later adopted in England by the Zurich Premiership.

In 2002 the Crusaders (Canterbury – New Zealand) became the first side to win the tournament undefeated in any of the matches on their way to the final, where they beat the 2001 winners the ACT Brumbies (Australia), 31-13.

In 2003 New Zealand's victory in the Tri Nations was preceded by a Super 12 victory for the Auckland Blues, 21-17, over their neighbours from Canterbury. The Brumbies won it again in 2004 but only kept the title for 12 months before the Crusaders won it back.

In 2006, Australia and South Africa each got one extra team in the competition and the competition became known as Super 14. The Crusaders have won the tournament twice since then, their victories split by a Bulls win in 2007.

Recent reports have suggested that South Africa may withdraw from the Super 14 post-2010. It has been speculated that South Africa may want to align themselves with European nations instead, because of the better time zone and travel issues. But in a later development, South African Rugby Union president Oregan Hoskins expressed his desire for two Argentinean teams to be included into the competition, expanding it to a Super 16.

Upsets

▲ England legends John Pullin (left) and Fran Cotton (right) were instrumental in the famous victory over New Zealand.

Upsets abound in the world of sport, that's what makes it great. Here are some of the most amazing from the world of international rugby...

AUSTRALIA 11 TONGA 16
Brisbane 1973

Many things are credited for Australia's rise in the rugby world. One of the most significant milestones in their recent history was their lowest point when Tonga humiliated them in 1973.

No one Down Under saw the defeat coming as the Tongans had limped through their Australia tour losing to New South Wales and the ACT. They arrived on the Sunshine Coast for a Test match few expected them to win. They had already lost the first Test 30-12 in Sydney.

Win they did though – in front of 9,563 fans at Ballymore – and they scored a staggering four tries to inflict the worst defeat in Australia's history. Australia even led, 11-8, going into the last 10 minutes.

The Australian rugby union, as we learn from the book *Wallaby Gold* never forgot the lessons from the defeat.

Peter Loane, from that team said; "It was also the start of something. We started looking seriously at things like the scrum and line-out.

"We always had brilliant backs but securing possession was the problem.

"But something had been started and 11 years after losing to Tonga, Australia won the Grand Slam (in Great Britain) and of course the World Cup in 1991 was the zenith."

NEW ZEALAND 10 ENGLAND 16
Auckland 1973

Victories in New Zealand are rare enough. For a side who had just lost to

▼ Legendary Argentinean number 10, Hugo Porta was instrumental in the South American Jaguars' extraordinary defeat of South Africa

Ireland and Wales and only beaten Fiji by a point it was surely a dream too far.

England's hopes were also dampened by three defeats in provincial matches in New Zealand.

The 1973 England side clearly hadn't read the script as John Pullin's side pulled off England's first victory in New Zealand for 37 years.

England scored three tries, through a sensational forward-powered performance, the decisive one coming from Tony Neary.

This great result wasn't even planned as the side was due to tour Argentina until the trip was called off under the threat of terrorist attack.

The book *Men in Black* saw England's achievement in the context of the All Blacks performance.

"While not wishing to detract from the merit of England's win we feel this must have been one of the most inept displays ever by an All Black team."

SOUTH AFRICA 12
SOUTH AMERICAN JAGUARS 21
Bloemfontein 1982

This was another example of the underdogs getting hammered in the first Test only to roar back in the second to beat their more illustrious opponents.

The Springboks had posted 50 points on the Jaguars in the first Test but in the return match they had planned without the genius of Hugo Porta.

The Jaguars were a team made up predominantly of Argentineans but they decided to forget about trying to win the battle up front in the second Test.

Porta, who many consider the greatest outside-half in the history of the game, took centre stage. It was one of the greatest one-man displays in rugby's history, as he scored all 21 points for the Jaguars. It was the record points total by one player against the Springboks.

With the South Africans banned from international rugby due to Apartheid it didn't rank as an official Test match but the South Africans and the South Americans regarded it as nothing less.

The Springboks made no changes to their team despite the initial 50-point hammering.

"The Springbok defeat in an often ill-tempered match is arguably the biggest upset in South African rugby history," explained Chris Greyvenstein in *Springbok Rugby – an Illustrated History*.

"Behind a vastly improved pack,

Porta proved that, at 31, he was still a masterful fly-half and he guided his band of no-hopers to a thoroughly deserved victory."

NAMIBIA 26 IRELAND 15
Windhoek 1991

You can take your pick from this shocking tour by the Irish, when they lost both games against Namibia. Although the second game was fractionally worse because at least for this Test they couldn't say they were taken by surprise.

The altitude of Namibia did contribute to the first Test defeat, 15-6.

This was no second string outfit either as 10 of the team that had played at Twickenham in the Five Nations were in the side and Ireland led 12-10 at half time.

Great Irish players like Nick Popplewell, Neil Francis (who went off in the second half with concussion), Donal Lenihan, Rob Saunders, Brendan Mullin and Jim Staples were in the side. Although they were without captain Phil Matthews because of a stomach upset.

But in Namibia they found a committed and passionate opposition that harried them from the start, and ran

in five tries, against two from Staples and Vince Cunningham for Ireland.

WALES 13 WESTERN SAMOA 16
Cardiff 1991

Wales finished third in the 1987 World Cup and with the pool stages in 1991 based in the Principality they were cast as one of the favourites to make the knockout stages.

They knew little about the men from the tiny island of Western Samoa but this incredible victory provided a platform to launch the careers of some of the island's great rugby stars.

When you consider the side that day included players like Mat Keenan, Apollo Perelini, Pat Lam, Steve Bachop, Brian Lima, Frank Bunce, and Peter Fatialofa the captain, it is perhaps a wonder how Wales got so close.

In many ways the victory did European rugby a big favour as we got

▲ The Welsh look singularly unimpressed by the Samoan haka prior to their shock defeat.

► Scott Gibbs on his way to scoring his famous try that sunk England's Grand Slam at Wembley 1999.

▼ Irish hero Eric Elwood is held aloft after Ireland's 17-3 victory over England in 1993.

to see those players in our leagues and they inspired a new generation of Samoans into the game.

"It's the greatest day in our lives. It's a great day in our rugby history," Fatialofa said.

Manager Tate Simi added; "To beat Wales at the Arms Park has always been a moment to cherish and this is very much so for the Western Samoan players."

IRELAND 17 ENGLAND 3
Dublin 1993

England fully expected to extend their six-year unbeaten run in Dublin when they arrived in 1993, only to be on the end of a shocking defeat.

Ireland fly-half Eric Elwood was the main destroyer scoring 12 points, Mick Galwey grabbing the only try, in the 80th minute, against an England team that had won back-to-back Grand Slams in 1991 and 1992.

The Irish swarmed over the England pack, getting on top and then disrupting the back-line.

The match signalled the end of an era for England with six of the side – Jon Webb, Stuart Barnes, Jeff Probyn, Wade Dooley, Mike Teague and Peter Winterbottom never playing international rugby again!

WALES 32 ENGLAND 31
Wembley 1999

England had watched France win back-to-back Grand Slams in 1997 and 1998 and it looked like it was going to be their turn in the last Five Nations of the decade.

Victories over Scotland, Ireland and France sent England to face Wales with the Grand Slam on offer.

Wales had endured an awful championship on the back of an awful decade and had lost to both Scotland and Ireland.

Added to that the National Stadium in Cardiff was a building site, due to the building of the Millennium Stadium and the game was switched to Wembley Stadium, London.

The Principality emptied to fill Wembley and they had a certain kicker called Neil Jenkins who was always capable of keeping his side in the game.

England – captained by Lawrence Dallaglio – were huge favourites and had raced into a 25-18 lead and should have tied the game up by half time. If it wasn't for Jenkins' boot they would have done.

In the second half England were still coasting and their confidence was typified in their decision to kick for touch late on instead of taking the points on offer, from the boot of Jonny Wilkinson, with the score 31-25.

A Wales penalty followed and Jenkins suddenly had the visitors back in their own half with the match almost over.

A rehearsed move involving Scott Quinnell and Scott Gibbs suddenly put Gibbs in the clear dancing through the England defence and over the line. Jenkins kicked the winning conversion and a nation celebrated!

SCOTLAND 19 ENGLAND 13
Murrayfield 2000

The bookmakers made England 1-12 to win this match at Murrayfield. For the second year running Clive Woodward's

▲ Andy Nicol secures the loose ball and an improbable victory for Scotland over England in 2000.

side arrived on the last day of the championship needing a win to clinch their first Grand Slam since 1995.

Woodward hadn't planned for an Edinburgh downpour and his side proved totally unable to cope with the rain or to change from one game plan to another.

It all started well, as it had done 12 months earlier against Wales, with a Lawrence Dallaglio try but they never put the Scots away and Duncan Hodge pounced with all 19 points.

England led 10-9 at the interval and after the match England coach Clive Woodward said; "It feels exactly like 1999 (when England lost to Wales). I can't say any more than that."

Scotland coach Ian McGeechan added; "My team had to play out of their skins and they did. They didn't let England settle."

VIIs (Sevens)

The shortened version of the 15-a-side game has its roots in Scotland, inspired by a butcher from Melrose, Ned Haig.

In 1883 Haig was looking for a way to make money for the Melrose club and hit upon the idea of varying the game. "Want of money made us rack our brains as to what was to be done to keep the club from going to the wall," Haig was later to recall.

"And the idea struck me that a football tournament might prove attractive. But as it was hopeless to think of having several games in one afternoon with 15 players on each side, the teams were reduced to seven."

The Melrose Sevens – which still runs today – proved to be a sensational success, not only saving the Scottish border club but inspiring a new avenue for the game.

Almost 2,000 people packed into the Melrose ground in April 1883 to see the Sevens contested by a number of Borders clubs.

The ladies of Melrose presented the Melrose Cup to the host club and the name has forever been entwined with Sevens. Even today the Rugby World Cup Sevens trophy is called the Melrose Cup.

Other Borders clubs like Gala and Hawick were quick to run their own Sevens tournaments but it did take many decades to take hold in the rest of the rugby world. The first World Cup was staged more than 100 years later.

After the First World War a Sevens circuit grew up in the Scottish Borders and to this day most of them still thrive, Sevens becoming a big part of the Scottish rugby culture.

Scotland – which staged that first World Cup in 1993 – has always remained the spiritual home of Sevens but closely challenging its place is Hong Kong. Perhaps the most famous Sevens event in the world, the Hong Kong tournament has allowed some big stars, including Jonah Lomu and David Campese their first taste of international rugby.

Hong Kong's annual jamboree kicked off in 1976 and in the early years the title was confined to Southern Hemisphere sides although England has produced an incredible hat-trick of wins from 2002-04.

The staging of the Five or Six Nations at the same time as the Hong Kong event had allowed the Southern Hemisphere their opportunity to dominate, until England started to prioritise Sevens as a feeder for the 15-a-side game.

Tokkie Smith was the Ned Haig of the 1970s driving the Hong Kong Sevens forward when he was greeted

with some scepticism in the early days.

Today the Hong Kong Sevens is one of the "must-do" events for rugby fans and players from all over the world.

The first Hong Kong Sevens, in 1976, attracted 12 teams and a one-day crowd of 3,000 but today the tournament stretches over three days and there are 40,000 fans (many of them in fancy dress) packed in on finals day.

"Basically there have been no excuses to miss the Hong Kong Sevens," explained John Blondin in his book *Rugby World Cup Sevens – Divine Intervention*. "A survey among the spectators will reveal that for many they

◄ Jonah Lomu with the 2001 Melrose Cup, so named after the Melrose Club, the pioneers of the Sevens tournament.

▼ Pat Sanderson of England beats the tackle of Pablo Gomez Cora of Argentina as England win the 2004 Hong Kong World Sevens.

▲ A young Lawrence Dallaglio powers forward to score a try during the 1993 World Cup Sevens final against Australia at Murrayfield.

have been attending for years as it is in their blood."

Hong Kong was the scene of the second World Cup Sevens in 1997, where Fiji took the crown, but the first World Cup was held in Murrayfield, four years earlier.

In 1993 an unfancied England team were victorious. England's lack of Sevens pedigree made them outsiders but as their team included players like Lawrence Dallaglio, Matt Dawson and Andrew Harriman it is no wonder they did so well! England beat Australia in the final.

Qualifying tournaments were needed in 1997 such was the interest being generated across the world.

In 1997 there was a public holiday declared in Fiji when they lifted the World Cup, in Hong Kong, beating South Africa 24–21 in the final.

In 2001 New Zealand became the third different winner, taking the trophy with a 31–12 victory over Australia, and in 2005 Fiji were again crowned champions of the Sevens world, beating New Zealand in the final 29–19. Fiji

also made the finals in 2006 and 2007 but were beaten by England and Samoa respectively. The trophy remained in the Southern Hemisphere in 2008 when New Zealand beat South Africa (making their first appearance in a Hong Kong final).

Former Australian Sevens captain Richard Graham explains the importance of the seven-a-side game in Gordon Bray's enthralling book, *The Australian Rugby Companion*.

Graham says; "Sevens is not, and never will be, a substitute for the 15-a-side game. Both have their own identity. "However, the famous Hong Kong Sevens tournament can certainly take credit for revitalising many of the skills of the longer game."

In 1999 the IRB harnessed the lure of Sevens with an international event or World Series. This Series attempts to take the game, rather like Formula One does in motor racing, all round the world.

The World Series has introduced the game into many new territories. Since its inception the World Series has been played in 16 countries across five continents and no fewer than 46 countries have participated.

New Zealand dominated the World Series in its early years, winning the first six competitions from 2000, confirming their domination of the series in 2005.

In England the magnificent Middlesex Sevens was almost one of the highest profile casualties of the professional era.

The Middlesex Sevens regularly attracted 60,000 people to Twickenham for an end of season party not bettered anywhere in Europe.

The English clubs demanded their own season finale and pushed the Middlesex Sevens into a start of the season slot that has failed to attract anywhere near the attention, crowds or standard of teams.

Rugby Sevens failed in its attempts to become an Olympic sport for the Beijing Games in 2008, but made its debut at the 1998 Commonwealth Games in Kuala Lumpur, where New Zealand won gold, repeating the feat in Manchester four years later and again, in Melbourne in 2006. Fiji picked up the silver medal in 1998 and 2002, England winning their first silver in 2006.

In Melbourne defending champions New Zealand have won their third consecutive gold medal with a 29-21

win. England were playing in their first Commonwealth Games gold medal match after earlier defeating Fiji 21-14. New Zealand made it to the final by beating Australia 21-19.

The biggest Sevens event in the world is the Rosslyn Park Schools Tournament which annually attracts over 3,000 schoolchildren from all over the world.

Colston's Collegiate School, Bristol made history in 2007 by becoming the first school ever to win both the Open (U18 Boys) and the Girls (U18) tournaments. The last day of the Tournament was broadcast live over the internet and it was watched in over 30 countries – highlighting the appeal of Sevens' rugby at grassroots level.

▲ Rupeni Caucaunibuca of Fiji breaks free to score a try during the Fiji vs South Africa Men's Rugby Sevens semi-final at the 2002 Commonwealth Games.

World Cup

As rugby union moved from being an amateur to a professional game in the 1980s it was inevitable that a World championship would be established and in the summer of 1987 the Rugby World Cup was born. Since then a tournament has been held every four years.

RUGBY WORLD CUP 1987
Winners: **New Zealand**
Venue: **Australia and New Zealand**

Sixteen teams were invited to enter the first Rugby World Cup in 1987 as the game embarked on a new era that many feared would end with that first tournament. But from humble beginnings the tournament has grown and grown.

Throughout history the New Zealand All Blacks had proved themselves to be the most successful team in the rugby world so it was fitting that it was their captain, David Kirk, who lifted the trophy after his side dominated the tournament.

From the very first match, which New Zealand won 70-6 against Italy, no one came close to stopping the All Blacks' relentless march to the title. Even in the final, against France they only conceded nine points!

Grant Fox was the New Zealand hero with 126 points and there was an unforgettable semi-final between France and Australia when Serge Blanco finished off a length of the field, injury time try as the Wallabies bowed out 30-24.

The home nations were sceptical about the concept but for Wales it represented their most successful World Cup to date as they finished third, beating England in the quarter-final, 16-3, and Australia in the third-fourth play-off, 22-21.

The games in Australia struggled to pull in the big crowds but in New Zealand, helped by the success of the hosts, things were different. The tournament brought 600,000 people through the turnstiles and a final profit of £1million.

RUGBY WORLD CUP 1991
Winners: **Australia**
Venue: **England, Scotland, Ireland, France and Wales**

With the success of 1987 behind them the International Rugby Board developed a far more ambitious tournament four years later, 40 countries starting a qualifying process that brought 16 teams to the Rugby World Cup finals.

The 1991 World Cup was significant for a number of reasons not least because it allowed Australia to emerge as a major force in the rugby world but

it also signalled the rise of the underdog. Western Samoa, as they were known then, changed everything we had believed about rugby's world order. They won a sensational 16-13 victory over Wales and only lost by nine points to eventual winners Australia.

The tournament opened in the magnificent setting of Twickenham; New Zealand winning the first match 18-12 against England. The reigning champion All Blacks failed to keep winning, though, bowing out in the semi-finals against Australia.

The Wallabies may have won the final, 12-6 against Will Carling's England, but they certainly didn't get things their own way. They needed an injury time try from Michael Lynagh to overcome Ireland at Lansdowne Road in the quarter-finals, 19-18.

But their ability to beat both New Zealand and England in the space of seven days made them worthy world champions, Australia scrum-half Nick Farr-Jones taking the Webb Ellis Cup from Her Majesty the Queen, after a final where prop Tony Daly scored the only try.

◀ David Kirk scores against France in the 1987 Cup final.

▼ John Eales and Tony Daley of Australia celebrate victory over England and a dejected Will Carling in the Rugby World Cup final of 1991.

► Joel Stransky
wins the 1995
World Cup for
South Africa with
an extra time drop
goal.

RUGBY WORLD CUP 1995
Winners: **South Africa**
Venue: **South Africa**

With Apartheid banished to the history books and the Springboks welcomed back into the rugby world there was only one place to hold the 1995 Rugby World Cup – South Africa.

This World Cup also benefited from being held in one country. When Nelson Mandela – the country's president – walked out on to Ellis Park to meet the teams for the final – New Zealand and South Africa – wearing a replica of South Africa captain Francois Pienaar's No 6 shirt the game had finally booked its place on the global stage.

Before the first match Mandela told the assembled players at the opening ceremony; "Your presence here affirms the unity in diversity, the humanity in healthy contest that our young democracy has come to symbolise. South Africa keenly appreciates your love and support. South Africa opens its arms and its heart to welcome you all."

The tournament was rugby's last as an amateur sport and it ended in sensational style, South Africa outside-half Joel Stransky kicking the winning drop goal in extra time to give his side a 15-12 victory over New Zealand.

England had come into the 1995 World Cup as one of the favourites. However, the Five Nations Grand Slam champions had to be content with fourth place after meeting a young All Blacks wing called Jonah Lomu in the semi-finals. The New Zealander trampled all over England's hopes with four amazing tries. Many people felt that England had played their "World Cup final" a week earlier when they beat Australia with a late drop goal from Rob Andrew, winning the quarter-final 25-22.

South Africa captain Francois Pienaar summed up the tide of pride and passion that had engulfed the Rainbow Nation during the tournament when, after the final victory, he said; "We did not have 63,000 fans behind us today, we had 43 million South Africans."

RUGBY WORLD CUP 1999
Winners: **Australia**
Venue: **England, Wales, Scotland, Ireland and France**

The 1999 Wallabies earned their place in rugby's history by becoming the first side to lift the Webb Ellis Cup twice when captain John Eales was handed the magnificent trophy from Her Majesty the Queen on 6 November at the Millennium Stadium.

The triumph not only represented their domination of the final, where they beat France 35-12, but their domination of the whole tournament. Where defence was supreme, they conceded just one try in the whole of their six-game campaign, and that to USA when they were giving a raft of their back-up players a chance to shine.

The final was in many ways an anticlimax to the France v New Zealand game, at Twickenham, which was without doubt one of the greatest games in rugby union history.

With the French battered by Jonah Lomu into a 14-point deficit they looked to be on their way out until they staged a sensational comeback to take the game 43-31, to make the final. It was French rugby at its best; full of flair

and with the focus of the attack coming from every position.

Lomu had once again been England's nadir scoring a try at Twickenham as the Kiwis won 30-16. That effectively knocked Martin Johnson's side out of the tournament. England's defeat ensured they finished second in their pool and were subjected to a midweek play-off before the South Africans inflicted the final blow in the quarter-finals.

For the first time none of the four Home Nations made the semi-finals, Ireland not even making the quarters and therefore having to suffer the ignominy of qualifying for the 2003 tournament.

RUGBY WORLD CUP 2003
Winners: **England**
Venue: **Australia**

The Rugby World Cup had been the domain of the Southern Hemisphere nations before 2003 when Clive Woodward's England shook-up the rugby world with a victory that catapulted his players into superstar status.

As it had done in 1995 victory

▼ Martin Johnson winning yet another crucial line-out for England in the 2003 Rugby World Cup.

▲ Action from the 2007 Rugby World Cup final between England and South Africa.

came down to a drop goal. Only this time it arrived from the right boot of Jonny Wilkinson with just over one minute of extra time to go in a pulsating final between England and Australia.

The full 80 minutes and almost all of extra time had failed to split England and Australia and they stood locked at 17-17 before Wilkinson struck to send the Webb Ellis Cup to Twickenham.

The 2003 tournament was widely acknowledged as the best World Cup to date with more spectators, a bigger television audience and a larger profit for the International Board to re-invest in the game than ever before.

RUGBY WORLD CUP 2007
Winners: **South Africa**
Venue: **France, Scotland and Wales**
Though France was the host nation

for the 2007 Rugby World Cup, several games were played in Edinburgh and Cardiff, and France found itself playing its quarter-final in Wales, against the All Blacks, who had started the tournament as odds-on favourites.

In a repeat of 1999, France gained a shock win, consigning the favourites to their worst result in World Cup history. France went on to lose against England at the semi-final stage. England, in turn, lost in the final to the Springboks, who equalled Australia's record of two World Cup wins.

England's Jonny Wilkinson became the highest overall point-scorer in World Cup history when he kicked all 12 points in England's quarter-final victory over Australia. He kicked a further nine points (including a 40-yard drop goal) in the semi-final and six in the final defeat to South Africa to bring his tournament total to 249 points.

In a change from the traditional format, the top three teams in each pool will qualify for the 2011 World Cup in New Zealand; previously, only the eight quarter-finalists gained an automatic place in the following tournament.

X-Codes

▲ Former rugby leaguer Jason Robinson scores England's try in the 2003 Rugby World Cup final.

Students of rugby league will have taken great satisfaction in the fact that the two tries scored in the rugby union World Cup final of 2003 were scored by former practitioners of the 13-man code.

Lote Tuquiri, the massive Fijian-born wing representing Australia, kicked off proceedings by beating his fellow convert, England's Jason Robinson, to a high ball to score first. But Robinson got his own back by touching down for the eventual winners. League followers would have taken little comfort from the way the flow of players from one code to another has been reversed in the last 10 years.

Tuquiri was one of three Australian backs hijacked from league who played in the final – Wendell Sailor and Mat Rogers were the others – while Robinson is perhaps the best player ever to negotiate the cross from the traditional game of the north of England to the 15-man contest.

A true rugby superstar in any language, Robinson's introduction to the England squad in the 2001 Six Nations was greeted with incredulity by some of the more experienced members of the press pack who follow the red-rose brigade around the international circuit.

Fast-forward to the Lions tour of 2001 when Robinson captivated some of the more one-eyed union followers with his devastating opening try in the first Test at Brisbane's Gabba. From then on Robinson was "one of us" and his impact in league's newly-paid brother has been immense.

Prior to 1995, it had virtually been one-way traffic. Union players struggling to meet the demands of juggling sport with a full time job and

▲ Jonathan Davies' first game back for Wales vs Australia in 1996.

and daytime training rather than trying to squeeze in shifts at the local bank, building site or casualty unit to make ends meet.

Welsh rugby union, in particular, has suffered hugely most notably when Jonathan Davies went north and Wales lost their only truly world-class back.

In 1989, after a superb career with Neath, Llanelli and Wales, Davies, to the consternation of the Welsh public, joined Widnes. Anyone who thought the quicksilver fly-half would be found out in league was swiftly put right as Davies added bulk to his speed and won 13 Great Britain league caps. In 1994, by now a Warrington player, Davies scored one of the most memorable tries ever seen at Wembley as Great Britain beat Australia 8-4 and was named "Man of Steel". He remains the best union player ever to make a success of league. Strangely, few of England's leading players ever seemed to switch codes – the dynamic wing Keith Fielding was a notable exception – but in the days of "shamateurism" there were ways and means of keeping them in union.

League's first real contribution to union, apart from a brief period in 1996 when players were loaned to the

family life were more than willing to take the cash to go north and play league. It gave them financial security and more importantly they were treated like professional athletes in that they had rest periods away from the game

15-man game, was on the 1997 Lions tour of South Africa. Players such as Scott Gibbs, John Bentley and Alan Tait had all played league and with professionalism in its infancy in union they showed the tour party the way. Martin Johnson's team were the first paid Lions and the input from the cross-coders was invaluable in securing victory over the Springboks.

One of the most recent high-profile and controversial converts was Andy Farrell, an undoubted rugby league superstar who announced his retirement from league to take on a new challenge with Saracens and the RFU. A series of injuries and accidents (including a car crash) meant that his debut in the 15-man code was delayed until 2006.

Despite his achievements in rugby league, questions were asked regarding his ability to change to a different sport at a relatively old age along with doubts about how much surgery he needed on his knees. There was also some criticism of the sum the then England head coach Andy Robinson was willing to pay for such a perceived risk, and whether such a substantial amount of RFU money could not be better spent elsewhere.

Farrell finally made his England

▲ Andy Farrell in action for Saracens, 2008.

debut at Twickenham after he was named at inside-centre in the first Six Nations game against Scotland. He impressed as a commanding figure in the back-line, especially since he left rugby league as a prop and played his early rugby union games as a flanker.

The 2007 World Cup saw Farrell

RFU Elite
Rugby director,
Rob Andrew.

playing in the unfamiliar position of fly-half against South Africa, in England's chastening group stage defeat. He was then brought on as a replacement against Tonga in his more usual position of inside-centre, and brought greater solidity to the midfield defensively, capping his impressive contribution with his first England try. However, after being picked for the quarter-final decider against Australia, he had to withdraw with a calf injury.

Whether we will see the likes of Farrell making the transition again is debatable following Rob Andrew's

decision in the autumn of 2008 that the RFU will no longer be funding big signings from rugby league.

This is not because the programme has been a resounding failure. There was, though, something rather unseemly about the rugby union nation with by far the most players at its disposal using its financial muscle to go after people who were undoubtedly New Zealanders, having already played a closely-related sport for NZ.

And while it was mildly hilarious to hear rugby league moans about sportsmen having the effrontery to change codes for money, not something about which it had entertained much moral distaste over most of the previous century, there is a strong case that a governing body – as opposed to individual clubs – is out of order when it goes after performers from another sport.

It won't, of course completely end inter-code transfers.

It will, though, be a matter for individual clubs to decide whether they want to take the risk always implicit in such a move, however evidently gifted the player, rather than being able to top-up with a Twickenham subsidy.

Young Ones

There are not very many records in rugby's history books that are out of the telescopic sights of Jonny Wilkinson, but even he will never be able to tick off the landmark of being England's youngest ever player on his bedroom wall-chart.

He got close though. His debut as a replacement against Ireland in 1998 came at the age of 18 years and 314 days and he was trumpeted as England's most fresh-faced representative for 71 years.

However, Wilkinson is not even the youngest fly-half to play for England as that honour goes to Colin Laird who pulled on the white No 10 jersey before running out against Wales on 15 January 1927, aged 18 years and 134 days, to help his team to an 11-9 win.

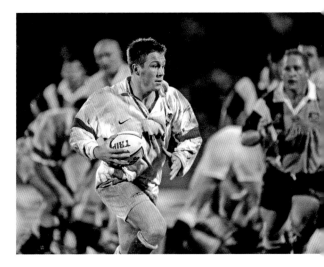

▲ Jonny Wilkinson in action against Australia aged just 19. Australia won 76-0 but Jonny was to get his revenge.

Wilkinson even had to settle for a place down the list of England's youngest captains when he was picked to lead the side against Italy in the 2003 Six Nations at the age of 23. Go back a mere 15 years and you will find that Will Carling was appointed captain at the age of 22.

Carling, who was in the Army before leaving to concentrate on his business career, was deemed officer material on and off the park by England manager Geoff Cooke who made him skipper for the home Test against the

▲ Will Carling, England captain at the age of 22.

 YOUNG ONES

Wallabies in 1988.

Carling was the youngest England captain for 57 years and barely out of short trousers, but he inspired his side to win 28-19 although the new boss had to be helped from the field after being knocked senseless with moments left. It looked as if the job was his for the next decade but he eventually returned to the playing ranks in 1996.

The New Zealand No 8 Taine Randell was entrusted with the captaincy of the All Blacks at the tender age of 21. And plenty of other countries have given the captaincy to a young shaver from the ranks over the years. The legendary Welsh scrum-half Gareth Edwards was tossed the metaphorical armband aged 20 and was the youngest rugby player to be awarded an MBE seven years later before, yes you've guessed it, Wilkinson got his gong at 23.

A fresh-faced Ken Catchpole led Australia on his debut in 1961 against Fiji and gave his side the mother of all dressing downs at the break after a poor first half. The Wallabies went on to win 24-6.

It must be something to do with scrum-halves who have to be pretty vocal carrying out their normal duties, but the hugely talented Nigel Melville was also England captain on his debut against Australia in 1984. He had the misfortune to run into the Grand Slam team of Mark Ella and Co who took the game 19-3. Melville's playing career was eventually curtailed by injury and he now plies his trade as a grey-round-the-temples coach at Gloucester and general-purpose rugby guru.

When the All Blacks made Jonah Lomu their youngest player by handing him his debut against France in 1994 aged 19 years and 45 days they knew what they were doing. The French actually won that day, 22-8, but the young Lomu was to terrorise defences for many years and went on to become rugby's first truly global superstar.

Winger Jack Hartley was 18 years and 18 days when he played for South Africa against Great Britain in 1891 whilst Claude Dourthe was 18 years and seven days when making his debut for France against Romania in 1966.

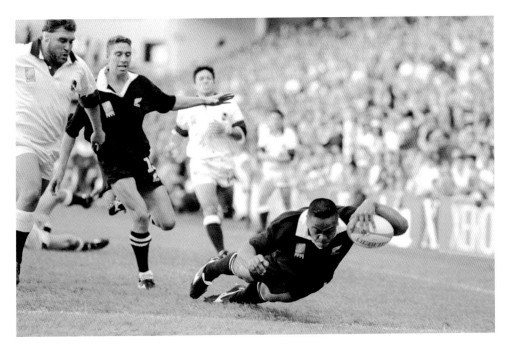

▲ 20 year old Jonah Lomu wreaking havoc on the England defence during the 1995 Rugby World Cup.

Scotland can lay claim to having the youngest international debutant in the shape of Ninian Finlay who was 17 years and 36 days old when running out against England in 1875. His countryman Craig Reid had also only been on the planet for 17 years and 36 days when lining up against the English in 1881, but as he had lived through an extra leap year the sticklers who compile the International Rugby Yearbook decided to make him the second youngest.

The magnificent Samoan centre Brian "the chiropractor" Lima, now 32, was a mere 18 years and 66 days when first playing for his country. He was still re-arranging opposition

▶ Samoan centre Brian "the chiropractor" Lima is still practising his art in 2003, 14 years after his debut. South African half-back Derick Hougaard will testify to that.

bones at the 2003 World Cup.

That tournament was notable for the appearance of a number of youngsters. Georgian scrum-half Merab Kvirikashvili was 19 when he headed to Australia and there were about 10 players who were aged only 20, including Wales' Jonathan Thomas, Samoa's Sailosi Tagicakibau and the United States' flanker Todd Clever. Joe Rokocoko was also 20 as were Schalk

Burger, the South African back-rower, Frederic Michalak of France and Italy's Mirco Bergamasco. And proving that if you're good enough you're old enough, Thomas, Rokocoko and Michalak were three of the stand-out performers of the tournament.

The England women's team fielded their youngest player in 2003 when the Bath schoolgirl and scrum-half Danielle Waterman, 18, came on as a replacement for Susie Appleby in the Grand Slam-clinching game against Ireland in Limerick.

Young players also have the chance to shine on the international stage in their own age groups. The Under-19s World Cup was first played in 1969 and France won the inaugural tournament in Barcelona before going on to win the next two as well. In fact, the French have absolutely dominated the tournament, winning it 10 times in a row from 1974 before Italy broke their grip on the competition.

Many stars of the future cut their international teeth in the tournament, but sadly the 2004 tournament was marred by the death of the Irish flanker John McCall of heart failure during a match against New Zealand. The Ireland team withdrew as a mark of respect to this brilliant, much-missed prospect.

The Under-21s World Cup started in 1995 and saw the Junior All Blacks run out winners in the final

of an event that has been dominated by the Southern Hemisphere sides. It is interesting to note that England, despite being a dominant force in senior international rugby, have a relatively poor record when it comes to the age-grow up events, even though many of their top players represented England at various stages before becoming international stars.

▼ John McCall (left) of Ireland makes a tackle during the IRB U-19 World Championship match against New Zealand played in Durban. McCall tragically collapsed and died of heart failure later in the game.

Zurich

For more than 100 years English rugby prospered without a league structure. The occasional cup competition came along but sides were happy with a series of hard-fought rivalries through friendlies. In 1987 that all changed with the establishment of the Courage Leagues.

These Courage Leagues developed when the title sponsorship was taken over by Allied Dunbar and in 2000 by Zurich, who established the top flight of English rugby as the Zurich Premiership.

At the birth of the English League structure two sides, Bath and Leicester, dominated proceedings. In the first 10 years their domination was only broken twice, and both times by Wasps.

Clubs weren't that keen on giving up all their longstanding friendlies in those early years and for the first six

seasons clubs in the top flight only played each other once. The structure developed into the fixture list we see today where sides play every other side in the Zurich Premiership twice a season, home and away.

Leicester were England's first official champions, in 1988, led by 126 league points from Dusty Hare, taking the title from Wasps, with a win on the last day of the season against Waterloo.

The remarkable Hare, who scored 368 points in all matches in that season, recorded 20 in their final 39-15 victory.

Leicester's first title didn't lead to domination by the Midlands side and within a year there was a new name on the trophy, Bath.

Bath's 1989 crown kicked off an incredible domination of the English game by the men from the Recreation Ground. They won, almost unbelievably, six titles in the next eight years. Wasps stopped their total domination in 1990 and there was a title for Leicester in 1995.

That 1989 title for Bath was accompanied by a Pilkington Cup final victory, at Twickenham, against Leicester, presenting Bath with the first league and cup double.

The legendary Bath team of the late 1980s and early 1990s went on to complete seven cup final victories and four successive Courage League titles between 1991 and 1994. They dominated English rugby in the way Liverpool had done before them and Manchester United after them in football.

The first of two league and cup doubles arrived in the 1988-89 season when club legends such as John Palmer, Jeremy Guscott, Andy Robinson, Tony Swift, Stuart Barnes, Richard Hill, Graham Dawe, Gareth Chilcott and Nigel Redman proved how good they were.

The league title in 1989 was won

with a 22-16 win over Nottingham, with two games to play. At Twickenham the double was completed with a 10-6 win over Leicester, in front of 58,000 fans, which was a world record for a club match.

The second double followed in 1992 when Stephen Jones, writing in *The Sunday Times* said; "Bath have the ability, when they need to, to rise to a different planet."

The arrival of professional rugby in 1995 saw a new team come to the forefront of English rugby and after Bath and Wasps won titles in 1996 and 1997 it was Newcastle's turn, in 1998.

Newcastle, coached by former England outside-half Rob Andrew, won their lone title by one point from

◀ Dusty Hare runs with the ball in the 1988 Courage League decider against Waterloo.

▼ Bath celebrate their fourth consecutive Courage League title in 1994.

▲ Pat Lam
celebrates
Newcastle's
Premiership
championship
after their victory
over Harlequins.

▼ Martin Johnson
rises high on his
way to captaining
Leicester to more
Heineken Cup,
glory.

Saracens, in a season when Samoan Pat Lam confirmed his status as one of the legends of the game.

Newcastle also became the only side to win the championship in their first season after promotion. Leicester handled the initial move to professionalism better than any other side in the Northern Hemisphere, reigning supreme in England and Europe, matching Bath's feat of winning four successive English titles.

Before the game turned professional Leicester battled for supremacy with Bath but once the Tigers had won their first English title, in 1999 they were unstoppable. They completed an incredible four consecutive English championship victories, starting in 1999, and lifted back-to-back Heineken Cups in 2001 and 2002.

Coached by Dean Richards and John Wells, in those four years of dominance, Leicester were almost unbeatable. They went 57 home matches undefeated in the Premiership between 30 December 1997 and 30 November 2002, when Northampton beat

them. Their incredible run included 52 successive wins.

Captained by Martin Johnson (See J for Johnno, Jason and Jonny) for all four of their titles, they lost only 14 of the 92 Premiership matches they played over those four championship-winning seasons.

In claiming that last title – in 2002 – Leicester had it almost won by Christmas, such was their domination. They lost just four times, scored more tries (72) than any other side and, significantly, conceded just 19 tries, 17 less than the next best, Northampton.

Chief Executive Peter Wheeler, a former club player, summed up the philosophy that underpinned their success. He said; "Nothing is taken for granted. We have no divine right to success. There's a good work ethic here, a self-critical attitude too. Complacency isn't tolerated. No one will tell you how good you are, only how to get better. We've never been a club to pat itself on the back.

"If you stand still then you're history." The four titles weren't the first time Leicester moved into the history books as they won three consecutive English Cup finals from 1979 to 1981.

In between Bath and Leicester's triumphs Wasps were the best team in England three times. In 2003 they lifted the trophy at the end of a new play-off system. From 2003 the top three sides at the end of the regular season go into a play-off. Second plays third, the winner taking on the side that came first, in a Twickenham grand final.

In 2003 this pitted the league winners Gloucester against second-placed Wasps, captained by Lawrence Dallaglio. The new system suited Wasps far better than Gloucester, who headed the league by 15 points, as Wasps built up a momentum towards the end of the season to take the final game, at Twickenham, 39-3.

Promotion and relegation from National One was established in the 2002-03 season, after many years of wrangling, when Bristol were relegated and replaced by Rotherham.

In 2005 Wasps won their third consecutive final, and in 2006 the league became known as the Guinness Premiership,

Sale winning their first English title, beating Leicester in the play-off final.

Leicester were back in the final the following year when they defeated Gloucester, who had finished first in the league table. Gloucester also finished first in the 2007-08 season but were defeated by Wasps in the final – Dallaglio's last game for the club before his retirement.

▼ Lawrence Dallaglio (right), the Wasps captain celebrates with team-mates Mark van Gisbergen (left) and Fraser Waters after winning the Guinness final match against Leicester Tigers in 2008.

Other books also available:

Available from all major stockists

Available from all major stockists

The pictures in this book were provided courtesy of the following:

GETTY IMAGES
101 Bayham Street, London NW1 0AG

COLORSPORT
The Courtyard, Lynton Road, London N8 8SL

MUSEUM OF RUGBY, TWICKENHAM
Rugby Road, Twickenham TW1 1DS

Creative Director: Kevin Gardner

Picture research: Ellie Charleston

Published by Green Umbrella Publishing

Publishers Jules Gammond and Vanessa Gardner

Written by Paul Morgan & Adam Hathaway. Updated by Jules Gammond